The Elements of Great Speechmaking

Adding Drama & Intrigue

Robert V. Smith

UNIVERSITY PRESS OF AMERICA,® INC.
Dallas • Lanham • Boulder • New York • Oxford

University Press of America,® Inc.
4501 Forbes Boulevard
Suite 200
Lanham, Maryland 20706
UPA Acquisitions Department (301) 459-3366

PO Box 317
Oxford
OX2 9RU, UK

Printed in the United States of America
British Library Cataloging in Publication Information Available

Library of Congress Control Number: 2004102470
ISBN 0-7618-2801-X (paperback : alk. ppr.)

The paper used in this publication meets the minimum requirements of American National Standard for Information Sciences—Permanence of Paper for Printed Library Materials, ANSI Z39.48-1992

To the Daughter of Mars

Contents

Preface

To be successful in the information age, professionals must be dramatic, interesting, and intellectually adventuresome communicators. As we compete in a world saturated with visually and intellectually stimulating multi-media messages, however, it is more difficult than ever to present ideas and initiatives in an effective and engaging manner. Enter *The Elements of Great Speechmaking: Adding Drama & Intrigue* (or *EGS* for short), which provides solutions.

Speeches and presentations represent crucial modes of communication for professionals. No longer, however, will a solid outline, some slides presenting compelling facts and statistics, and an impressive amount of knowledge of a single subject be enough to present ideas convincingly. Increasingly, leaders in a variety of fields will be expected to be both learned and intellectually adventurous. As technology continues to make the world into our neighborhood, professionals must illustrate their love of learning and their eagerness to continue learning as they simultaneously find ways to integrate this learning into the workplace. Additionally, they must find ways to prepare and deliver speeches and presentations in new and compelling ways.

EGS provides today's professionals with the tools needed to communicate effectively and successfully in the 21st century. More specifically, *EGS* is the only book available that teaches professionals how to think in more innovative ways and how to infuse their speeches and presentations with the crucial components of drama and intrigue.

The *EGS* book, which offers a host of useful resources and references, utilizes a four-fold approach. Section I guides you through the initial planning for presentations, illustrating the importance of factors including audience make-up and audience expectations. Included here are tips for early "detective work" that may spark possible ideas for dramatic and intriguing approaches and materials. Section II provides essential tools and materials for enhancing the elements of drama and intrigue that are so necessary for effective presentations. These tools and materials run the gamut from quotes to historical and literary allusions to art works to sartorial accessories and props, with advice on how best to use them. In Section III, blueprints are offered for crafting talks, from outlining presentations, to using the tools and materials discussed in Section II, to working with PowerPoint™ software. Section IV contains tips and suggestions for making dramatic and intriguing presentations—from knowing how to successfully begin your talk to assessing the venue for the presentation to thinking about what to wear to using props and multi-media to dealing with questions and comments.

Throughout, *EGS* is embedded with Uniform Resource Locations (URLs) that facilitate access to artwork, graphics, and other materials that may be considered for possible "fair use" in presentations. A series of extensive Appendices, representing a wide variety of rich source materials, is also included—from self-deprecatory jokes to quotes to historical and literary allusions to suggestions for use of sartorial accessories and props.

The professional who reads *EGS* and embraces its philosophy and methods will assuredly become a more dramatic and intriguing speaker. As a result, this newly empowered speaker will become not only more self-confident but also more effective as a professional and a leader.

Charles Francis, owner and editor of the information resource Internet service, *IdeaBank®*, noted the following in the June 2002 Issue of the *IdeaBank Newsletter*:

"A new survey reveals that 96 percent of executives report some level of anxiety when speaking in public and that 21 percent suffer from extreme anxiety.

According to the survey, women are three times more likely than men to experience high public speaking anxiety.

An important finding for *IdeaBank* subscribers is that 62 percent of the executives surveyed said they combat fear and anxiety by preparing thoroughly."

Guiding professionals through the successful preparation of speeches and presentations that are original, effective, and make a difference in today's world is exactly what *EGS* does.

EGS differs from other "How To" books on public speaking in a number of ways. First, it does not assume that the reader is clueless about giving speeches and presentations. It does assume that many of its readers have some experience with public speaking and that if they are not already speakers themselves, they will have had many opportunities to witness some very good speeches. Additionally, *EGS* stands apart from other work in the field as a result of the extensive resource material the book provides. This material has the kind of strong interdisciplinary emphasis and intellectual breadth that are crucial for effective speechmaking in today's information age.

EGS has been written for mature professionals who are interested and eager to take the next step in their professional development. It is for readers who are interested in using their speeches and presentations to most effectively deliver ideas and initiatives and for those who know that successful public speaking can set them apart in today's competitive world. Because of its balance of philosophy, pragmatism, and substance, *EGS* will hold great appeal for the educated professional. Its readers will especially include mid- and upper-level professionals in higher education, the professions, and governmental and non-governmental organizations. It will also appeal to managers and executives in the corporate sphere.

For professionals who employ speechwriters, *EGS* can help improve the dialogue between these parties and more effective speeches will inevitably result. Speechwriters, in turn, will benefit from *EGS* and its messages.

I have made hundreds of presentations before professional and service organizations, legislative committees, university and foundation governance and advisory boards, faculty and higher educational administrative officials, college-age student and parent groups, K–12 students and teachers, and business and economic development groups. These hundreds of speaking engagements in a variety of venues have been testing grounds for the successful public speaking materials, approaches, and methods described in *EGS*.

So now, I offer these tools, materials, tips, suggestions, and approaches that should help enliven and enrich your presentations. I also hope you will consider—if you are not already—getting intimately involved in presentations you give; that you will find—as I have—an interesting set of challenges and an intriguing set of rewards that await the speaker who is not only orator but creator or co-creator of her or his material. Indeed, I have found that the speech writing and preparation efforts described throughout this book can become some of the most effective tools for the continuing education of 21st Century leaders. Thus, I hope that this book will provide the possible inspiration for readers to adopt new speech writing approaches in their own careers. In all that you do—in planning, evaluating tools and materials, crafting, and making presentations—I wish you: *bonne chance* as a speechmaker.

Acknowledgements

Throughout *EGS*, there are references to notable speakers and colleagues who have influenced my thinking about speech writing and speechmaking. I hope that my attributions will serve as honest appreciation for their notable efforts. Others' efforts and influences are less apparent but also very much appreciated. My agent, Cecelia Cancellaro (Idea Architects; http://www.ideaarchitects.com), was most helpful in crafting the book proposal and offering editorial advice on several sections of the final work. Her encouragement and efforts, in general, contributing greatly to this project.

I am also grateful to several colleagues at the University of Arkansas: 1) Carolyn Allen (Dean of Libraries) and her colleagues provided reference help on several occasions; 2) Bob Brady (Chair, Department of Communication) and Doyle Z. Williams (Dean, Sam M. Walton College of Business) offered useful suggestions and encouragement; 3) Larry Malley (Director, UA Press) was helpful in locating a high quality agent.

Throughout my professional career, various administrative assistants, secretaries, and program assistants have contributed to my speech writing and speechmaking efforts, sometimes typing quotes and notes, other times assisting with PowerPoint™ production or projections. I single out for special commendations: Kathie Biondi, Donna Blacker, Lynda Carey, Linda Dizney, Judy Okita, Dottie Williams, and Marilyn Wilson.

Charles Francis (Owner of *IdeaBank*®, http://www.idea-bank.com/ib/html/) went well beyond the call of duty in uncovering publication leads and encouraging the project. Ultimately, Nicole L. Caddigan (Acquisitions Editor for the University Press of America) saw merit in this manuscript and I am grateful for her insight and support.

I leave for last, the person who always comes first in my life—Marsha June Smith, who is much more than wife or help-mate. She is my confidante, my muse, and my unstinting supporter, and a contributor to several sections of this work, not least of all the portrayal of her art in Chapter 5 and her photographic contributions found in a number of figures and on the book cover.

Section One

PRESENTATION PRE-PLANNING

You receive an invitation to speak before a civic or professional organization or department within your place of employment. You agree to speak. Ideas begin to race through your mind on how you might approach the challenge. You will want to assess the landscape, review the tools and materials available, craft the talk, and finally, become prepared to present your handiwork. Your pulse accelerates as you begin the efforts. You anticipate greater and greater levels of satisfaction as you choose tools and materials; as you begin the actual construction of the talk; as you choose approaches that will insure a dynamic performance. All you need now is to commence the process. So, let's begin!

Chapter One

Assessing the Landscape

Nothing interests people more than themselves. This is not meant to be a cynical statement. Rather, psychologists know that when we look at group photos in which we are included—our image is the first that we search for among the subjects. The orientation towards self is also true of groups and their identities. Thus, when addressing an audience, a presenter's most important preliminary task is to find out about the group's interests and affiliations, the expectations and occasion for the presentation, and the possible uniqueness of its timing and location. With this information, you can begin identifying the tools and materials that will insure that your presentation is not only informative but captivating as well.

INTERESTS AND AFFILIATIONS OF THE AUDIENCE

After accepting an invitation, you should begin seeking information on the apparent expectations of the audience along with contextual and other background intelligence that might enhance bonding with the audience—in special ways. For example, an invitation to address an induction ceremony for a high school branch of the National Honor Society (NHS) should immediately prompt a visit to the national organization's website (see *n. 1*). This research would reveal that the organization espouses the values of Character, Leadership, Scholarship, and Service. Thus, a presentation to this group would quite naturally include a discussion of one or more of these values, depending on the proposed length of the talk. For example, a 15- to 20-minute slot would not allow one to do justice to more than one or two of the NHS values.

FURTHER EXPECTATIONS AND OCCASION FOR THE PRESENTATION

But, let's backup for a moment. Before going off in a preconceived direction and despite what might seem obvious about audience expectations, probe the person or persons making an invitation to determine the precise expectations—if any—of the audience or group.

Sometimes, the expectations are unusual. Take, for example, the time I was asked by a representative of a state chapter of the Association of College and Research Librarians to make a presentation to their group on the "image of librarians." You can probably imagine the stereotypical traps I had to avoid in tackling such a topic. Seriously, the prospective audience's preferences for your presentation are important and not always obvious. These factors must be taken into account as you select your topic as well as the material for the talk.

Sometimes, however, the invitation is couched in terms of "speak on something related to your professional expertise or experience" or "share with us some perspectives that might assist our organization or its members in performing their jobs." This kind of open-ended invitation can very well give you the options or "hooks" for engaging the audience in special ways, since you may now more creatively approach the challenge of choosing dramatic and intriguing material and tools. For example, the NHS talk alluded to earlier was given at a large high school in Fort Smith, Arkansas and was developed according to the following outline:

- Introduction—a lesson from President Thomas Jefferson
- Research & scholarship definitions
- How does scholarship relate to learning?
- How does research & scholarship make a difference?
- Suggestions for becoming a scholar

The talk—using PowerPoint™ (ppt)—began dramatically with an allusion to Thomas Jefferson and his scholarly interests that helped set the goals for the Lewis and Clark Expedition (the so-called "Corps of Discovery"). There is more about this topic in Section II but for now, let me note that the initial "hook" was this: Jefferson set the United States on a scholarly course when he admonished Meriwether Lewis and William Clark to not only map their journey but write about flora and fauna and send back specimens (preserved and alive) to Washington for inspection. Jefferson also craved insight about Native Americans and their languages and culture, as well as assessments of the potential of an America with extraordinarily expanded borders. Indeed, Jefferson's thirst for scholarship laid the groundwork for education as we know it today—education enriched immensely by the scholarly passions of teachers and professors.

I continued my NHS presentation with examples of prominent individuals whose lives have been driven by a passion for scholarship. The examples included great scholars I have known such as Norman Borlaug (plant pathologist and winner of the 1970 Nobel Peace Prize for wheat varietal work that led to the "Green Revolution"), Barbara Harbach (musicologist and renowned harpsichordist), and Everett Ladd (prominent social scientist and long-time Director of the Roper Center at the University of Connecticut). The presentation ended with suggestions to students for becoming scholars, including:

- Becoming a keen observer
- Studying broadly—the liberal arts
- Finding focus
- Developing analytical skills
- Seeking interconnections or integrated understanding
- Nurturing skeptical optimism
- Developing good communication skills
- Developing personal information resources
- Using the Internet wisely
- Seeking wisdom

The talk—by all indications—was a success. The success reinforced the importance of relating to audiences through their personal or group-oriented aspirations and goals. And, the approach is not necessarily limited to the two examples given thus far.

To broaden our perspective a bit, let me offer succinctly a few more examples of how I have used audience interests and affiliations in speech preplanning in a wide-array of situations.

- During the seventies and eighties, I was invited to speak at several pharmaceutical firms (e.g., Schering Corporation [Bloomfield, NJ], Pfizer Inc. [Groton, CT], Riker Laboratories [St. Paul, MN]) about research that colleagues and I were doing on the use of microorganisms to produce human metabolic derivatives of drugs and other chemicals. In all instances, attempts were made to draw analogies between our work and products marketed by the individual companies.
- As a consultant to the Upjohn Company (Kalamazoo, MI) during the early eighties, I gave a series of talks that ranged from specific scientific presentations (e.g., development and testing of novel drug-delivery systems) to professional development topics (e.g., scientific writing, time management). In

all cases, the topics and material development were customized according to feedback from a manager assigned to my efforts by the divisional vice president who had hired me. An embarrassing anecdote relative to one of these presentations is contained in Chapter 13.

- While employed at the University of Texas at Austin, I served for eight years as chair of a campus-wide committee charged with reviewing research protocols involving human subjects. The experience of reading more than one hundred protocols per year and articulating committee decisions to researchers helped me develop expertise that led to a series of presentations on the historical, legal, and ethical aspects of human subjects research. These presentations were made before audiences varying from graduate students in areas such as education and nursing to a multi-institutional hospital review board to a conference group consisting of academicians, industrial researchers, and U.S. Food and Drug Administration officials. In each case, material was added or modified to engage the audiences in special ways (e.g., incorporating information on University-specific procedures in talks given on campus). The intriguing use of popular cultural references in these talks is described in Chapter 6.
- During the decade of the nineties, when I was the chief research officer at Washington State University, I worked collaboratively with my counterparts at the University of Washington to develop and propose an Advanced Technology Initiative (ATI) to the Washington State Legislature. ATI was proposed as a multi-million dollar project designed to recruit and retain highly talented researchers who could help stimulate new high technology business ventures in the Evergreen State. In a series of presentations to Washington House and Senate Committees (e.g., economic development, higher education) we were responsible for making the case of the positive economic impact of university-based research. The presentations were designed to offer convincing economic arguments and embodied some intriguing uses of props that are described in Chapter 9. In Chapter 13 I offer some advice on desired attire when addressing legislative committees.

Once adequate attention has been given to audience interests and affiliations, it is then desirable to determine if location or timing of a presentation suggests dramatic or intriguing approaches.

LOCATION AND TIMING OF THE PRESENTATION

Location—yours or your audience's—may offer special opportunities and must be carefully considered as you plan your presentation. When I was doing pharmaceutical research as a professor and drug research institute director at the University of Texas at Austin, I was often given opportunities to speak at conferences and meetings—sometimes in unusual places. During the Texas years (1974-85), I developed a talk and set of slides on the history and geography of Texas. This presentation was often more popularly received than my scientific presentations, such as the time I spoke to the staff and guests in a national park in Croatia in 1981.

It became apparent to me during my travels "as a naturalized Texan" that people all over the world wanted to know about this fascinating place in America. Indeed, my "Texas history and geography talks"—interlaced with references to popular cultural perspectives (e.g., remember the widespread interest in "Who shot JR?") were a hit everywhere I went. References to other places I have lived (e.g., Washington, Idaho, Connecticut, and Arkansas) present slightly greater challenges to heighten interest, but I think you will see—as we proceed through this book—that there are intriguing ways to generate interest in your background, your perspective, and your locale—whatever it may involve or wherever it may be. Also in Chapter 4, I offer several examples of how locations and timing may influence presentation preparations relative to the use colors, flags, and territorial representations in talks.

To summarize, affiliations of audiences, the occasions for presentations, and the uniqueness of locations or timing of talks are key initial factors in the planning of dramatic and intriguing presentations. In the following section, we'll move to the next step and explore how best to select the most effective tools and materials for your presentations. Sources and suggestions including humor, quotes, anecdotes, proverbs, stories, logos, seals, and references to artistic, historical, literary, scientific and technological scholarship and research, as well as sartorial accessories, artifacts and props, will be discussed in detail. These are the tools and materials that will bring your presentations to life by providing drama and intrigue, which are crucial and often overlooked elements in the preparation and delivery of the very best speeches and other presentations.

NOTES

1. The National Honor Society is actually the National Honor Society/National Junior Honor Society or NHS/NJHS, which are registered trademarks of the National Association of Secondary School Principals (NASSP) (http://www.nassp.org/index.htm—file).

Section Two

TOOLS AND MATERIALS

Understanding the challenge that lies ahead, you begin assembling and assessing the tools and materials that will be helpful in preparing a dynamite presentation.

The tools and materials for drama and intrigue are many. Some are good. Some are great. Some fall flat. Experimenting, testing the impact, and determining the different effects of presentation tools and materials offer exciting challenges and rewards—for you and your audiences. So let's see what's out there from humor to art to literature to science to sartorial accessories and props, among others.

Chapter Two

Humor, Symbolism, Irony, Paradox, Satire, and Double Entendre

Be of good humor but be careful of humor in presentations. Humor is the one element of presentations that has the greatest danger of failing. Besides being misinterpreted, humor can offend or it can just flat-out fail unless you are very good at it. Joan Detz (2000), well-know speechmaker and coach, also offers this advice. Thus, exercise care when incorporating jokes or other humorous references into presentations. Be wary of humor that may be interpreted as raunchy or insulting to audience members.

Having grown up in the New York metropolitan area, I once had a know-it-all sense that led to gaffes, which did not play well—particularly west of the Hudson River. Marx Brothers-type insults—that I so fondly enjoyed from childhood—were not well received when used before different audiences. For example, when introducing a speaker with background from a seemingly Podunk place, I might offer the quip: "Well we'll forgive him or her for that!" Unfortunately, audiences may contain people who live or have lived in "Podunk-like places" and the reference is ill received. In contrast to put-downs, self-deprecating humor such as that used by notable speakers inside and outside of the performing arts—are well received.

Woody Allen and Bill Cosby are masters of self-deprecating humor. So is Grady Jim Robinson (2000, 2001)—humorist and storyteller extraordinaire—who uses his son-of-a-coach failures at sport—augmented by voice mimicking—with great aplomb. But, unless you have such professional skills, consider humor sparingly and make sure it is genuine, spontaneous, and self-deprecatory. With these caveats in mind, some self-deprecating ideas and comments are offered in Appendix 1.

Many of the ideas in Appendix 1 represent "seeds" because self-deprecating humor is best when it seems or is in fact spontaneous. Thus, ideas for self-deprecatory quips are often suggested by introductory comments. For example, for the professional referred to as being on a career "fast track," you might offer, "Thanks for the reference to my being on a fast track; but, I assure that there have been some derailments along the way." Thus, the ideas and suggestions in Appendix 1 seed self-deprecatory humor that is crafted "on the spot" but humor that will work even if you are not a skilled comedian.

Akin to self-deprecatory humor, symbolism, irony, paradox, satire, and double entendre can be used effectively to add drama and heighten audience interest. To illustrate the uses of these tools and attendant materials, references are offered below to talks I have given on the "Art and Science of Professional Development and Productivity in the 21st Century Workplace," "The Promise of a New Position," and "The Many Faces of Scholarship."

The art and science talk has been given in different formats for staff professionals and faculty members but had similar outlines. Because of the unique nature of these particular talks, some background and explanation is in order relative to the use of art history to highlight and enrich the "science of personnel management."

If you have given talks on management, you know the kinds of subjects they contain—subjects such as team building, continuing education, mentoring, and professional development, to name a few. Most professionals have attended such presentations through short courses, national or regional conferences, or guest presentations at one's place of employment. Basically, the material is not inherently enthralling. Thus, it occurred to me that seemingly unexciting points could be illustrated more intriguingly through references to great art and great artists. For example, a point about continuing education might be illustrated with Pablo Picasso's work "Girl Reading at Table" with some references to the symbolism of cubist art as noted later.

An outline of one of the professional development talks is provided below to assist the illustration of the use of symbolism, irony, paradox, satire, and double entendre in presentations.

THE ART AND SCIENCE OF PERSONNEL DEVELOPMENT AND PRODUCTIVITY IN THE TWENTY-FIRST CENTURY WORKPLACE

Topic Outline: The Twenty-first Century Workplace, Personnel Development, and Productivity

The Twenty-first Century Workplace

- Individual *versus* Team Efforts
- Diverse and Non-Hierarchical

- Teaching and Communication Skills
- Advanced Portals
- The Virtual Workplace

Personnel Development

- Intellectual and Social Development
- Continuing Education
- Professional Organizational Involvement
- Mentoring
- Managerial Involvement

Productivity

- Facilitating Routine Tasks
- Building Innovation into All Efforts
- Cross Training
- Strategic Planning—Vision, Mission, Goals, and Objectives
- Quality Control and Quality Assurance

In Appendix 2, each topic and sub-topic noted above is described in greater detail and Uniform Resource Locators (URLs) are given for the one or more works of art and in most instances, pictorial representations of artists. The choices of art works and artists were made to illustrate points and to introduce the elements of symbolism, irony, paradox, satire, and double entendre. For example, the topic outline slide—containing a title ("Outline") and three major topic headings ("Twenty-first Century Workplace," "Personnel Development," and "Productivity")—incorporates a reproduction of a four-part block-like work of Mark Rothko (see Appendix 2) in part to symbolize the four elements of this slide and in part to serve as an introduction to the talk drawing on some well-known art history. Specifically, Rothko wished to have his works displayed so that one could view them up-close and indeed in a manner to suggest the possibility of proceeding into them as one might enter a portal. Thus, the Rothko work introduces the notion that one is passing from the outline to the substantive portions of the talk in an intriguingly symbolic manner (Rothko 2001).

Symbolism was also used to illustrate the need for continuing education in personnel development. In the appropriate slide, Pablo Picasso's "Girl Reading at a Table" (see Appendix 2) is used to symbolize the need for innovation in continuing education by drawing upon a known feature of the cubist art form. Specifically, the cubist's attempt to portray in two dimensions, three-dimensional elements of a subject—particularly elements that not usually in the viewer's grasp (Hoving and Wyeth 1999)—symbolizes the innovation that managers and individuals need to incorporate into continuing education plans. Isn't this a more interesting way of expressing the ideas imbedded in the terribly over-used phrase, "thinking outside of the box"?

The use of irony and paradox are exemplified in the slide for Individual *versus* Team Efforts, through famous works by Caravaggio and Georges de La Tour. The slide is intended to illustrate the importance of team efforts in the 21st Century workplace but with the caveat that work in teams may bring out petty jealousies or disagreements that must be avoided. Carrivaggio's and George De la Tour's depictions of cardsharps and their accomplices duping innocent participants in group play (see Appendix 2) offer ironic and paradoxical examples of the dark side of team efforts. These artistic examples also allow the point to be made—dramatically—that managers must be conscious of the dark side of group interactions to prevent their adverse effects on organizations.

There are several satirical allusions in the professional development talk, although my favorite involves the use of Grant Wood's most famous work, in the slide pertaining to Manager Involvement. Here, the balanced involvement of the manager—steady but not micro-managing—is illustrated with a representation of "American Gothic" (see Appendix 2)—one of the most well recognized paintings of the 20th Century. Few people know that the models for the farmer and his spinster daughter are the unmarried sister (Nan Wood) of Grant Wood and the artist's and his sister's dentist (Dr. Mckeeby). One cannot resist the humorous and incongruous association of a pitchfork and the normal modus operandi of dentists. Likewise the sour expression on the farmer's face provides a humorous reference to what personnel would rather not have among supervisory managers.

For those interested in the remaining allusions to art works and artists chosen for the topics of the "art and science" talk, complete information is provided in Appendix 2.

While the term "double entendre" is often used to portray the mixing of racy and prosaic meanings, I have used it in talks simply to convey "double meaning"—in an intriguing way. To illustrate the use of double entendre, I am offering some description of a talk—"The Promise of a New Position." This talk was developed as a introductory presentation for a wide variety of groups following the acceptance of a position as provost or chief academic officer at a major research university. The talk and a companion paper, which was published on the university's website weeks before arrival "on the job," served as a harbinger of my management style and philosophy. In this case, the double entendre included in the title offers the inherent message of the talk; namely, the "promise" or "promises" of a new position involves not only the "promise" for the person holding the position but, the "promise" that the new person must make to the community he or she serves.

To elaborate just a bit more, a new post offers personal promise for novel challenges and rewards. On the other hand, and more importantly, it offers new opportunities for service. In the case at hand, service to the university's academic community—its faculty, students, and staff. More specifically, a provost should serve the academic community by: (1) encouraging faculty, student, staff, and program development, (2) evaluating accomplishments, and (3) representing these accomplishments to the university's constituents—within and outside of the institution. And then, as noted to my constituents: My *promise* to you is that I will honor these commitments to the best of my ability while insuring the values of quality, trust, and integrity—in all that I do.

All of us have had to start new professional positions. For me, it has happened six times. I have found, however, that the "promise of a new position" approach—incorporating the double entendre of "position" in a paper and a corresponding talk—helped me make the most satisfying "running start" in one of the last positions of my career.

Besides the "new position" presentation, double entendre has been used effectively in talks about diversity and the academic workplace. For example, I have used the talk, "The Many Faces of Scholarship" to offer the message that the richness of scholarship in its many forms—from science and technological research to historical scholarship to creative performance—are enhanced by the diverse views and perspectives offered by a diverse faculty and student body.

The word "diversity" can also be used in its double and multiple meanings relative to graduate education. Thus, I have talked several times to prospective graduate students about diversity in terms of diverse programs, diverse approaches, and the diversity that should be sought among students in the modern academic environment.

The use of humor, symbolism, satire, irony, paradox, and double entendre often involves drawing from personal assessments and syntheses. As we look towards the next topic—quotes, anecdotes, proverbs, and stories—we'll be thinking about ways to use the thoughts of others and elaborations of personal experiences to add drama and intrigue to presentations.

Chapter Three

Quotes, Anecdotes, Proverbs, and Stories

The use of quotes, anecdotes, proverbs, and stories bring audiences close to interesting people and ideas—famous and not so famous. That is the great attraction of these speechwriters' tools and materials. But, there are caveats that merit attention before adopting these tools and materials in a wholesale manner. Here are some cautions that may be used to guide the use of quotes, anecdotes, proverbs, and stories:

- Be cautious of using quotes without context. The place, setting, and circumstances of a quote may alter its meaning immensely. If used without considering context, quotes can be turned into "misquotes."
- Be wary of quotes by politicians. One of the oddities of the lives of prominent politicians is that they may or may not be the source of inspiring rhetoric. Often, politicians' expressions are more reflective of the thoughts of speechwriters or political parties than public servants.
- Be judicious about citing material from collections of quotes. There have been instances of misquotes being perpetuated through such collections. For example, the often quoted, "Nice guys finish last."—attributed to the well-known manager of the once Brooklyn Dodgers (and the New York Giants, Chicago Cubs, and Houston Astros), Leo Durocher, is actually a journalist's (and perhaps his or her editor's) contraction of a much longer set of sentences that bare only a slight resemblance to the pithier quote (Yagoda 2002). The truncated expression appears as such in *Bartlett's Familiar Quotations* (1992). Other misquotes, false attributions, and indeed, fake quotes can be found in a wonderful work by Boller and George (1990).
- Always identify the individual being quoted and avoid anonymous quotes.

- Consider the earlier elaborated guidelines (e.g., avoiding humor that is offensive) when adopting anecdotes containing humor.
- Be careful of sources of proverbs. An alleged Scottish proverb may show up in another collection as a German or Italian proverb. The coincidence may or may not reflect accurate antecedents and may or may not make the proverb "ring true."
- Be thoughtful about the often proffered advice regarding the crafting and telling of stories. Storytellers are frequently liberal in their use of fabrication in the crafting of tales. If developed under the rubric of material appropriate for a novel, novella, or fictional short story, there are no problems with such an approach. However, if portrayed as a "true personal story," fabrication can get you into trouble.

With the above cautions in place, let's consider the use of quotes, anecdotes, proverbs, and stories—one-by-one.

QUOTES

There is almost nothing better than a great quote to infuse drama and intrigue into a speech. The content of the quote—its relevance to the talk, its poignancy, and its effective expression—all add greatly to the message of a talk. Now, if you can also find an appropriate quote from someone who is instantly recognizable, you have a winner. Better still, if the person is famous and related in some way to the audience, you've got a knockout. If all of the above are true—and you have met or know the person quoted, you've got a blockbuster.

Having known the great American physicist and colleague of Einstein, John Wheeler, I have been able to impress many an audience of physicists and other scientists by referring to his myriad words of wisdom. One of my favorite Wheeler quotes (Swainson 2000) is, "Time is what prevents everything from happening at once." I have used this quote on several occasions as an ending line of an introduction to a meeting or conference with the tag line, "Fortunately we have time in a generic sense, but it is now the appropriate time to begin our conference."

I have also been blessed to know Norman Borlaug, the 1970 Nobel Peace Prize winner, honored for his development of dwarf wheat that made the "Green Revolution" possible. Quoting or paraphrasing Borlaug's thoughts have been great hits with agricultural groups. I would love to brag some more, but it would be boorish. The take-home message, however, is this: "If they had something relevant to say, are eminent, and you know 'em—quote 'em."

Now, even the most prominent reader will not know great numbers of sages, thus, you have to rely on context, content, relevance, and the potential impact of quotes—adopted from whomever.

Anyone who has any experience writing speeches knows about sources of quotes. Standard references such as *Bartlett's Familiar Quotations: A Collection of Passages, Phrases, and Proverbs Traced to Their Sources in Ancient and Modern Literature* (1992) and *The Oxford Dictionary of Quotations* (1999 and Ratcliff 2001) are well known. Less well known, but representing a collective treasure house of quotes with interesting twists, are *The Great Quotations* and *The Great Thoughts* works of Seldes (1983 and 1985). There are other quote-laced references available on CD Rom, such as *The Columbia World of Quotations* (Andrews, Biggs, and Seidel c. 1996). I have also subscribed to an Internet service known as IdeaBank® (see Bibliography), which is a great source of quotes and other material as will be noted subsequently. Other websites for quotes include QuotableQuotes (http://www.quotablequotes.net/) for quotes in general and a site specifically containing quotes by notable women (http://www.geocities.com/~spanoudi/quote-09.html).

In addition to standard references, I collect quotes. I have cataloged quotes from every book and many articles I have read since 1985. The "collection process" causes me to be a pretty slow reader but the underlining and highlighting has led to a File Pro™ database containing more than 900 entries.

Then there is the quote that you vaguely remember but cannot find in the book that you may have read many years ago. Fortunately, there is a way around this dilemma without having to re-read the entire book. You can now subscribe to services such as Questia (see Bibliography), the latter of which allows you to download any number of books from a digitized collection of more than 70,000 volumes (in 2003) along with hundreds of thousands of journals and articles. Once downloaded, of course, you can use a computerized "find function" to help locate a "lost quote."

As to specific quotes, I wish to first share a set of future-oriented quotes, which I have used in talks. If you are like me, you have found people to be fascinated by presentations about the future. What could be more intriguing especially if the future vision—as Charles Kettering would comment—"is where we will spend the rest of our lives"? (see below). Again, if you are like me, you'll probably be tempted to craft talks about "The Future . . . of this or that." Or, as we will see in Section III, craft significant components of talks devoted to the future.

When giving future-oriented talks, it is also fun to point out that there is a World Future Society (http://www.wfs.org/) that was started in the United States in 1966 and now has 30,000 members in 80 countries around the world. So much for having to prove that people love to think about the future!

But, back to future-oriented talks. Following are a set of quotes that offer a engaging way of beginning such talks, especially if the quotes are revealed in dramatic fashion. If you are using PowerPoint™ or slides, partial quotes can be offered with an implied question to the audience to see if members can complete the quotation. For example, President Abraham Lincoln said:

"The best thing about the future is that it comes . . . (one day at a time.)"

Below are the other partial quotes that can be used to stimulate audience intrigue. Context and quote completions appear in parentheses.

- (The future is) "where we will spend . . . (the rest of our lives.)"
  Charles Kettering (American twentieth century engineer-inventor and founder of the Dayton Automotive Laboratory Company [DELCO])
- "The future ain't . . . (what it used to be.)"
  Yogi Berra (former NY Yankee catcher and "king of malapropisms")
- "It is difficult to make predictions . . . (especially about the future.)"
  Niels Bohr (Danish physicist colleague of Albert Einstein; also attributed to Enrico Fermi, [Italian physicist and University of Chicago-based leader of the Manhattan Project], and Samuel Goldwyn [movie mogul])
- "We have to worry . . . (about the future.)"
  Isaac Asimov (science fiction writer and futurist)
- "If you do not think about the future, you . . . (won't have one.)"
  John Galsworthy (English novelist and playwright; author of *The Forsyte Saga*)

Audiences love this little game of trying to finish the "future quotes." Indeed, if you use them in the prescribed manner, you will have people coming up to you after a talk asking that you review the quote endings. Now that's heightened drama and intrigue!

Appendix 3 contains additional quotes that I have consulted many times for occasions that are likely to occur in the life of active speechmakers. Perhaps the shared quotes will be of use in your oratorical life.

ANECDOTES

Analogous to quotes, anecdotes offer great opportunities to exemplify or embellish points. Anecdotes can be obtained from the literature or sources such as IdeaBank®.

Personal anecdotes are often most effective, particularly if they happen to bridge your interests and the experiences of your audience. For example, I often speak before groups containing academics and other professionals who are authors of books and papers. Writing accomplishments are heady experiences, but when I refer philosophically to placing such experiences in perspective, I frequently share an incident that happened to me several years ago.

I am proud of a research management book I wrote in the eighties, especially since it was published by the University of Texas Press and appeared in two editions. During a faculty visit on the Washington State University campus in the early nineties, I encountered a biological chemistry graduate student who asked, "Are you the author of the book, *Development and Management of University Research Groups*?" Yes, I said proudly. "Well" he said, "I just bought a copy of it on sale at the University book store. I paid a nickel for it!" So much for fame and fortune.

In my area of higher education administration, I often wish to share anecdotes with faculty and students about experiences that may inspire scholarly work. One of my favorites involves Barbara Harbach—a musician especially noted for her performances of works by women and one who was rated in *Keyboard* magazine as the second best harpsichordist in the world. Harbach's dedication to scholarship on women's roles in music composition comes from a negative experience. She relates how—in the eighties—she was astounded by an off-hand comment by a male music historian: "Women have never composed anything at all, and if they did, it certainly wouldn't be any good." That assertion sent Harbach off on a quest for music by women, which has led, by way of the British Music Library, to the founding of a publishing company and scholarly journal (*Women of Note Quarterly*; http://www.vivacepress.com/) and many scholarly presentations, which have helped illuminate the wonderful works of Hildegard Von Bingen, Fanny Mendelssohn, Clara Wieck Schumann, and many others.

While anecdotes provide opportunities to share short vignettes and descriptive incidents, proverbs provide even shorter messages—but messages with unique power for transmitting meaning.

PROVERBS

As noted earlier, proverbs obtained from collections may sometimes have muddled references as to sources but, proverb content and context frequently provide clues to the authenticity of origins. Chinese proverbs, for example, frequently have the "ring" of Taoist thought.

I like proverbs because of their ethnic origins and the likelihood that members of almost any audience in many countries—especially the United States—will have at least some members who will relate to their use in an especially fond way. When you think about it, you need all the friends you can get when giving speeches.

Kidding aside, I have used proverbs frequently, as transition elements, themes, and in crafting endings for talks. Some of my favorite proverbs are contained in Appendix 4. Many are available through IdeaBank® and I have included several of varying ethnic origin that could be used in myriad talks from memorial services to professional development presentations. The particular proverbs offered in Appendix 4 were principally accessed through IdeaBank® using the key words: death, leadership, life, learning, or wisdom. And, even a cursory review will reveal several of noteworthy value as dramatic and intriguing transition or concluding elements.

As suggested earlier, there are other uses of proverbs. For example, the English proverb, "Something old, something new, something borrowed, something blue," will be recognized as one that is commonly referred to in connection with women's wedding garb. However, the references, "old," "new," "borrowed," and "blue" can also be used as theme words in presentations. During such presentations, I also enjoy sharing an anecdote about the famous bandleader, Glenn Miller, who used them as a guide to song medleys, and according to Bob Kase at the University of Wisconsin-Stevens Point, particularly when introducing his singer Johnny Desmond, who was famous for a rendition of *Serenade In Blue*.

Another special favorite is the Japanese proverb that can be used most effectively to close a talk, and if you are speaking to a group connected with marine studies, fisheries, or fishing—all the better. The "proverbial ending" goes like this: "There is a wonderful Japanese proverb that states 'Fish die by the mouth.'—I shall not! Thank you and good day."

STORIES

As many have learned from reading Joseph Campbell's *Hero with a Thousand Faces* (1968) and derivative works, stories represent powerful tools and materials for connecting with audiences. And, stories that contain archetypal elements will evoke particularly meaningful bonding between a speaker and members of the audience. One of the strongest archetypes is that of the hero (used here in a gender neutral sense) and the hero's quest which typically involves three basic elements: (1) departure from home or other comfortable setting, (2) tackling challenges and succeeding, and (3) returning triumphantly—literally or symbolically. Other archetypal themes may stress elements or events such as (Wilson 1998):

- Genesis-type stories focusing on the creation or early development of families, firms, institutions, or organizations

- Coming-of-age stories particularly those involving travel to exotic destinations
- Apocalyptic stories wherein people or places are threatened with dire circumstances
- Stories that begin with the power of a skill, knowledge, or talent
- Tales that relate to the extraordinary influence of a mentor or friend

Indeed, these classic archetypal forms can even be effectively adopted as the outline for a presentation as will be exemplified in Section III. For now, imagine stories about famous personages, notable incidents, or organizational developments—in terms of venturing forth, facing challenges, and accomplishing results and you will have a winning formula.

Many, I am sure, have heard some of the great storytellers of our time. I include on my list: Maya Angelou, Leo Buscaglia, Joseph Campbell, and Grady Jim Robinson, all of whom I have seen in person or experienced through audio or videotape. These and other charismatic storytellers draw from literature sources but also blend literature references in uniquely personal ways. For example, who can forget Leo Buscaglia's many stories about his Italian parents who displayed a stereotypically passionate devotion to him while he was growing up. The stories Buscaglia developed in his speeches, whether they included the generosity of his father or the doting of his mother—ring true. They touch our heartstrings because of their universality, their personification of kindness, and their triumph over adversity. These are the kinds of elements that need to be sought in stories that are shared with audiences. These elements are winners!

If you would like to hone your story telling talents, I recommend books by McGuire (1998) and Robinson (2000). Also, the Technology for Learning Consortium Inc. has a website with some helpful tips on story telling (http://www.techforlearning.org/storytelling.html).

Having considered the use of quotes, anecdotes, proverbs, and stories in speeches, let's now take a different turn and consider more subtle—yet interesting and effective elements for imbedding drama and intrigue into presentations.

Chapter Four

Colors, Flags and Territorial Representations, and Logos, Seals, and Symbols

It has been noted that the prominent early 20th Century modern artist, Wassily Kandinsky, as an adolescent, had a conviction that colors have mysterious lives of their own (McMullen 2003). Colors, whether they are part of a PowerPoint™ presentation or included dramatically and intriguingly in sartorial accessories, can be used effectively to make points. Beyond colors—flags and territorial representations, and logos, seals and symbols can be used effectively in presentations, especially PowerPoint™ presentations, and thus, each of these sets of tools and materials deserve separate attention.

COLORS

If you are a devotee of late-night American television you have probably noticed how David Letterman's musical sidekick, Paul Shaffer, uses color in his clothes and accessories—including his eyeglasses—to draw attention to his performances. In women's fashion, the comings and goings of colors have been legendary during the past half-century and perhaps since antiquity. Descriptions of colors and their relative relationships in the rainbow can add metaphorical "color" to your life, including speeches and other presentations.

You may recall from basic physics or natural science study that the order of the colors of the rainbow are remembered through the acronym R-O-Y-G-B-I-V (red, orange, yellow, green, blue, indigo, and violet). It is an ordering that I have used to organize many things in my life from neckties to folders used to hold daily papers. Accordingly, the red folder denotes Monday, orange Tuesday, yellow Wednesday, green Thursday, blue Friday and indigo and violet—weekend days. I even color coordinate with coated paperclips but enough about my fetishes. Besides sharing these idiosyncrasies (or "idiotsyncrasies" as Leo Gorcey of Bowery Boys' fame was known to say) occasionally with audiences, I have used colors to make other more important points.

For example, I admire the color "heliotrope" which has some specific meaning at the University of Arkansas (Smith 2002). Accordingly, I have had many opportunities to challenge "Razorback audiences" with the question "What is heliotrope?" The question, regardless of the audience, provokes blank stares or quizzical looks. When told it is a "color," few people can envision its color characteristics.

According to the *American Heritage Dictionary*, "heliotrope" is "a moderate, light, or brilliant violet to moderate or deep reddish purple." My favorite permutation is the latter, which is best exemplified by the color of most common eggplants. Indeed, when I share my fascination of heliotrope, I often suggest to someone that the next time they are in a grocery store or farmer's market that they hold an eggplant up to the light. As it is turned from side-to-side your eyes experience a type of double refraction or birefringence, in which you see the red and violet hues of the vegetable's surface almost simultaneously.

Remembering the colors of the rainbow through the previously noted acronym ROYGBIV, we are reminded that "heliotrope" portrays simultaneously colors from the opposite ends of the spectrum. In a sense, therefore, heliotrope captures the ends of a continuum in an especially beautiful way, and in a way that helps it serve as a metaphor for many of the things we value at universities. But, more about this point—in a moment.

To pursue the significance of heliotrope to the University of Arkansas (UA)—note that it was considered for adoption as the school color prior to 1895. But, as described in a UA magazine published in 1895, "After a short but fierce contest between the partisans of heliotrope and cardinal, the latter triumphed, and it now holds a conspicuous place on the apparel of the students and professors." The UA magazine writer went on to mention, "Since we have a magazine, a college color, and a college yell, we feel that we are in some measure catching up with the times." (Hale 1948.)

In the course of UA school color choices and university name and mascot changes between 1894 and 1916, heliotrope became lost to antiquity. However, I have tried to resurrect an interest in heliotrope at the University of Arkansas and elsewhere not only for its historical interest but also for its appeal or what may be portrayed as the "power of heliotrope."

Heliotrope may be thought of as a metaphor for the power derived from bringing differences together for strength, longevity, and wisdom. The "power of heliotrope" is imbued in the strengths of our country and our universities nation-wide through the diversity of our students and faculty—their ideas and accomplishments.

The "power of heliotrope" is akin to the power of innovation and creativity that mark many university-based endeavors. Examples include the uniting of scientific fields, such as that of biology and chemistry, which has given us biochemistry and biotechnology—scientific areas of importance in efforts from crop development to disease prevention. Other examples include the balancing of meaning and sounds that add so much to notable poetry and the scripts for great films and plays. I also think of blending different views and perspectives that inspires the development of good public policy. In short, the "power of heliotrope" is a vital component of all of the nation's universities (and, probably many other institutions), which are known for discovery- and scholarly-based learning.

I then offer one additional thought: the power of heliotrope parallels the power of the liberal arts. Before he died, Milton Rokeach—one of world's most famous social scientists—reminded millions that wisdom is an understanding of our universe through the arts and sciences. Just as heliotrope blends differences in a beautiful way, wisdom offers insight from what are often perceived as dramatically opposed perspectives. This is true power—embodied in the "power of heliotrope."

When speaking to UA audiences, I end the heliotrope story with the challenge: if you would like to discuss the "power of heliotrope" sometime, watch for me at a future Razorback event. I'll be easy to spot—in my heliotrope jacket! And, I do indeed have a heliotrope-colored jacket for such speaking events. But, I will have more to say about sartorial accessories later. For now, let's pursue further the use of colors and color-references in talks, lest I leave this topic with what some may believe to be a narrow and specific example of somewhat limited value.

Kandinsky was on to something about colors. But, rather than pursuing his ideas of colors having "lives of their own," we can consider the virtues and characteristics commonly associated with the colors of the rainbow. Appendix 5 contains a listing of colors and associated disciplines, symbols, and virtues that may be useful in crafting analogies and metaphors. Note particularly in Appendix 5, the inclusion of colors associated with various disciplines (e.g., lemon yellow—library science, pink—music)—colors that are gloriously worn during college commencement exercises.

You can undoubtedly imagine how the color references can be incorporated into talks—through the use of PowerPoint™ presentations and analogies to content. I also find that references to colors are most powerfully used in connection with flags and their colors, especially when coupled with references to states and nations familiar to audiences.

FLAGS AND TERRITORIAL REPRESENTATIONS

I love flags—including flags of states, nations, and organizations, and those used for utilitarian purposes (e.g., signal flags). I love the shapes, colors, and symbols imbedded within flags. I love to study the connections among flags and geographical places and peoples they represent.

There are many ways to use flags—or representations thereof—to create drama and intrigue in presentations. The first thing to do—of course—is to find context and connection to your audience. Actually, this is quite easy even in the United States because many people do not understand the symbolism of their own state's flag, no less that of other states and nations. Particularly when speaking at international venues, flags can be used in very special ways.

Consider, for example, a recent opportunity I had to speak before a town council in Italy. The occasion was a ceremony in the Tuscan community of Cervara di Roma, a small village in a mountainous area about 40 miles northeast of Rome. I was representing the University of Arkansas and a partnership we were proposing with this medieval hamlet to craft summer internships for UA architectural students. The drama of the event was heightened by the fact that it occurred on September 22, 2001, just eleven days after the horrible events of 9-11. My wife and I had been in Italy since September 10, 2001 and had experienced the wonderfully heart-felt expressions of the Italian people for Americans and America following the terrible events of September 11. I anticipated no less on this sunny Saturday morning and the Commissioners and other town officials who spoke prior to my remarks were as passionate and genuine in their supportive comments as those we had encountered earlier that week.

The stage of the Cervara di Roma town hall displayed full-sized versions of the red, white, and blue American flag and the red, white, and green Italian flag. The juxtaposition of these beautiful standards prompted the thought that the flag colors—their similarities and differences—might be used in a dramatic way to make the point about the solidarity suggested by recent events. Thus, I proposed to the mostly Italian audience—that at this moment in history—the solidarity between America and Italy are represented by the colors embodied in our *two* flags: white for the genuineness of feelings we have toward one another and red for the courage the citizens of our two countries have displayed on many occasions as allies in common battles, including the new war against world terrorism.

As for the different colors, I suggested that the natural beauty and pristine environment of Cervara di Roma were symbolized by the American flag's blue—as in the blue sky—and the Italian flag's green—as in the wonderful surrounding flora. Take my word for it. There were few dry eyes in the audience, after drawing these analogies.

I have had several other occasions to use flag references, albeit in less dramatic circumstances, but with intriguing and what I thought—powerfully symbolic meaning. For example, I co-moderated (with the president of a university in Ghana) and gave a plenary talk at a sustaining agriculture conference in Cote d'Ivoire in West Africa in 1995. The conference participants were mostly governmental agricultural officials from nations in Sub-Saharan Africa. Thus, I had a special opportunity to craft linkages to audience members through art incorporated into the talk's slides, which were prepared before the common use of PowerPoint.™ Today, the task would be facilitated by art work readily available through the world wide web (e.g., *World Factbook*, see Bibliography).

In any case, on each slide for the talk, printed material was superimposed on individual outlines and flag facsimiles of countries of participants at the meeting. Thus, audience members could feel a special identification with the presentation material—well beyond its substance. One drawback to this approach—of course—is that you may miss someone's country. But, a preliminary apology for possible omissions usually suffices.

I have used permutations on the Cote d'Ivoire talk when speaking in the United States. Of course, in recent years, I have enjoyed imbedding representations of the Arkansas flag and the state's seal in PowerPoint™-assisted talks presented about topics related to the University of Arkansas. The symbolism of the gesture, especially for groups outside of the University, is that the University serves the people of the State and the meaning of this symbolism is not lost on audiences. This practice represents a straightforward example of flag use when speaking in your home state. But, for Americans, there are even more creative ways of using flag and territorial representations in talks given beyond your state.

When I was living in the State of Washington, I served on a gubernatorial commission devoted to enhancing biotechnology-based industry in the state. The commission was quite successful in its efforts and captured the imagination of other states including the State of Alabama where I was asked to speak about the work of the Washington Commission before an audience of business, government, and university leaders who wished to consider possible parallel efforts in their great state. I saw this opportunity as one to not only share pertinent ideas but also to brag a bit about the beauties of my then home State of Washington.

Again, this was before the time of PowerPoint™ technology, but through some photographic craftiness, I was able to superimpose text on a template including an outline of the State of Washington. The composite images of text and Washington State's outline were then superimposed on photographic images of locales in the State. The latter images were obtained from state tour guides. The total effect—text on beautiful photos of places in the state—bordered by the state's outline—was marvelous. Audience members were quite impressed especially since I could—during the presentation—point to the places on the state's outline, which were represented in the background photos. If you have been to the Olympic state, you know of its great natural beauty—which enhanced the presentation in an especially dramatic and intriguing manner.

As noted in Section I, I was also a naturalized Texan for eleven years of my life. During those times, I used to embellish talks with background pictures taken from the many beautiful and interesting places in the Lone Star State.

The Washington and Texas experiences can be emulated. Regardless of whether you are from Washington, Alabama, Texas, New York, Nebraska, or other U. S. state or nation, you should be able to find interesting permutations of the examples noted above to add drama and heighten intrigue in your presentations. You'll probably learn some things in the process and your audiences will love it!

LOGOS, SEALS, AND SYMBOLS

If you want to engage an audience in a special way, consider adoption of a logo, seal, or symbol of an organization or organizations that may be represented among the audience. The adoption can be affected by incorporating representations of the logos, seals, or symbols in the title or other slides. Another "trick" is to use logos, seals, or symbols from your and an organization visited—on alternating slides. This is a particularly effective way of emphasizing a possible partnership that you may be encouraging between your organization and the one at which you are speaking.

Logos, seals, and symbols can also be used effectively when welcoming people to your institution or organization. For example, in title slides you can juxtapose a picture or other instantly recognizable logo, seal, or symbol of your institution or organization with that of the institution or organization of your guests. This tactic provides the clear signal: while you are here you are "at home." As the Mayor of Rome wrote to Americans who were local hotel guests following the September 11, 2001 catastrophic terrorist attacks in the United States, "at this very moment . . . you can consider Rome as your home."

An additional good use of logos, seals, or symbols is in emphasizing different missions of an institution. At the University of Arkansas, for example, we consistently offer the message that we want to strike a healthy balance between academic and athletic efforts at the University. Thus, we commonly make PowerPoint™ presentations where the slide template contains the logo depicting the "Old Main" tower—symbol of the academic excellence at the University—and the well-known Razorback—our University's athletic mascot.

The use of logos, seals, or symbols in presentations parallels somewhat our earlier discussion of the use of art images, which are considered more extensively next—along with works of art.

Chapter Five

Artwork and Works of Art

Earlier in these pages, we discussed using art to illustrate humor, symbolism, irony, paradox, satire, and double entendre. You should now be able to let your imagination run wild about allusions and parallelisms that might be used through art representations in myriad talks. When calling upon your creative instincts and capabilities, you are only constrained by your knowledge of art history, which may or not be well developed. If your art history knowledge is well developed—fine. If not, you might consider developing a greater avocational interest in art history as I did several years ago. As you consider incorporation of art into talks, however, don't limit yourself to representations. You should also consider the less obvious but extremely effective use of actual art objects in your presentations.

Picture this. You come out onto a stage to give a talk. The stage is stark naked except for a podium on one side and an easel on the other. The easel holds an *objet d'art* covered by an opaque cloth. You can make quick reference to the easel or allow its mysteriously covered object to remain cloaked and ignored throughout most of the presentation. But the audience will notice.

Many have experienced the above scenario at award ceremonies where relatively standard plaques or framed awards remain cloaked until the awards are made. Adoption of this practice with *objets d'art* during talks adds the additional drama of the unexpected.

Surely you will unveil the *objet d'art* at some point. But what might it involve? How might it relate to the presentation? You can imagine such anticipatory thoughts in the minds of audience members. And, it's true—the drama works. I've used this tactic and observed its success in many of my own presentations throughout the years.

Now, you need an intriguing, relevant, and poignant *objet d'art* to unveil. You might start by looking through your family's collection or borrowing a work owned by the firm, institution, or organization you serve in your professional life. The *objet d'art* need not be an original, but if you do have access to an original work its uniqueness only enhances its use.

Let me offer two examples of art-enhanced presentations from my own speaking experience. The first emanates from a eulogy presented following the untimely death of a dear friend and colleague just a few years ago. His name was Bob Gray and he served at different times during his lifetime as Dean of Fine Arts at the University of California, Los Angeles (UCLA) and the University of Connecticut.

Akin to his eighteenth century sea-going namesake who was the first American to circumnavigate the globe, Bob Gray circumnavigated and contributed greatly to the world of the fine arts. He had earned a Master of Fine Arts degree from Yale University and received, during his life, medals from three countries honoring his contributions to the visual arts—particularly painting. He was a man who numbered among his artist and art patron friends and acquaintances such notable figures as Victor Borge, Frank Capra, Sean Connery, Katherine Hepburn, Ron Howard, Sol Leavitt, Jack Paar, Robert Redford, and Raymond and Beverly Sackler. He truly lived a "life of the arts."

The above allusions to Bob Gray were used to eulogize him following his sudden death during the summer of 1999 (Smith 1999). But, the *piece d'resistance* of the eulogy was a watercolor painting that Bob had done of my wife's French bulldog, Monsieur Hercule Poirot—named after Agatha Christie's famous Belgium French detective. Bob had been fascinated by Poirot's ability to move his ears in thirteen different directions. In a painting of Poirot that he created and gave to my wife just a few months before his death, Bob added an inscription that exemplified this fascination (see figure 5.1).

The Poirot painting was covered by a cloth and placed on an easel several feet from the podium where I eulogized Bob Gray before a very large group of his family and friends. The eulogy included background on my wife's and my relationship with Bob and his wife, Connie, who partnered in crafting *objets d'art* as gifts and thank you cards that they presented and sent to hosts during and after dinner parties, including dinner parties in our home. After sharing some contextual remarks about one of these gifts—the Poirot painting—I ceremoniously walked across stage, unveiled the 30" × 22" work and read the inscription aloud—with the best French accent I could muster: "Sept [7], huit [8], puff, puff" (moi, Poirot, I show the oh, so many POSITIONS-DES-EARS. where was I?) "onze [11]—eh—non [not]—eh—douze [12]—eh—eh . . . . . merde [shit]." The audience broke into laughter—certainly some of it including comic relief. The eulogy ended with the thoughts that Bob Gray was a one-in-a-billion and a true *tour de force*. The words were well received and the impact of the *objet d'art* was clearly significant.

Fig. 5.1. Bob Gray, *Monsieur Hercule Poirot,* 1999, 30 × 22 in. (76 × 56 cm.); photo by Russell A. Cothren

I have used *objets d'art* in many other presentations with similar salutary effects. These art-enhanced efforts have been aided in part by works created by my wife, who happens to be an artist. One of her paintings, in particular, has been used to illustrate the concept of consilience; a term coined by the Pulitzer-prize winning biologist E.O. Wilson (1998).

Consilience, or the unity of knowledge, is the concept that all fields or disciplines can be connected when crafting a unified understanding of our natural and cultural worlds. Wilson illustrates this point by allusion to the Greek myth of Theseus and the Minotaur.

Briefly, Theseus was engaged by King Minos to slay the half-bull half-man Minotaur—a monster who was responsible for the deaths of countless Grecian citizens. For Wilson, Theseus is humanity, the Minotaur a metaphor for human irrationality, and the Cretan labyrinth—the home of the Minotaur—the challenge we face in conquering irrationality by connecting cells (metaphors for disciplines or areas of study) in just the right pattern to achieve understanding. Of course, the story is incomplete without Ariadne, the amorous daughter of Minos, and the weaver of the golden thread that allows Theseus—the hero—to descend into and return from the labyrinth—after slaying the Minotaur. Ariadne's thread, therefore, becomes the metaphor for consilience or the notion of connecting all fields of scholarship to achieve holistic understanding.

I have used Wilson's concept of consilience in many talks about interdisciplinary and integrated scholarship. The talks are ended by an unveiling of the painting depicted in figure 5.2—a painting based on the well-known Greek myth and created by my wife, Marsha June Smith.

Fig. 5.2. Marsha June Smith, *Ariadne's Thread,* 1996, 18 × 14 in. (46 × 36 cm.); photo by Russell A. Cothren

When preparing your own presentations, be sure to look around and consider connections that might be used to engage audiences in dramatic and intriguing ways through *objets d'art* that may be available to you.

There are additional strategies for using art in talks, including art embodied in neckties, lapel pins, and other sartorial accessories, as will be pointed out a bit later. For now, however, let's look at how other fields related to the liberal arts, including the humanities, natural sciences and technology, and social sciences, may be used as valuable sources for tools and materials that will greatly enhance the elements of drama and intrigue in your presentations.

Chapter Six

History, Literature, and Popular Culture

We take on huge areas of learning when thinking about historical, literary, and popular cultural references as tools and materials for talks, but I am going to do it anyway. In so doing, I hope to offer some approaches you may not have thought of before. Because of the enormity of the topic, we'll take the elements of it—one at a time.

HISTORY AND HISTORICAL REFERENCES

If you have had similar experiences to me, you have often heard people say, "I hated history in high school." Or "I hate to memorize dates." Yet, I have found that far greater numbers of people have a fascination with history, particularly if you can relate it to them and their place in time—in intriguing ways. As support for this proposition, I ask you to consider the enormous popularity of historians such as Fawn Brodie (e.g., *Thomas Jefferson*), David McCullough (e.g., *John Adams*), and Barbara Tuchman (e.g., *Guns of August*), among many others. I refer particularly to David McCollough, who is not only a fine historian but also a great speaker who makes history live in wonderfully engaging ways. The popularity of books by Brodie, McCullough, and Tuchman, as examples, makes the point about the attractiveness of history, especially among audiences of educated people.

I have also found that historical references appeal to audiences of varying educational background, particularly through temporal links. For example, you can use historic events of the day to spark interest in particular portions of your presentation. This approach involves using a source such IdeaBank® (see bibliography) or the *New York Times* website (http://www.nytimes.com/

learning/general/onthisday/) to determine historically important events of the day of your talk and relating these events—in dramatic and intriguing ways—to the theme of the presentation. Table 6.1 contains some examples of this approach—examples taken from welcoming remarks or comments I have made to groups about impending events.

Besides the use of daily historic events, you might look for opportunities to refer to important recent or forthcoming anniversaries of events that have

Table 6.1. Use of Historic Events of the Day to Add Drama and Intrigue in Presentations

Presentation	*Date: Historical Event*	*Remarks or Context*
A New Year's social event honoring the accomplishments of senior University of Connecticut academic staff	January 9: Date that Connecticut become the 5th State to enter the Union (1788) and the date of the Ancient Roman "Agonium Festival"—in honor of Janus, the god of Beginnings, Doorways, and Archways	Comments were offered on the interesting coincidence of the evening's event with an important day in the history of the State of Connecticut. Also, an allusion to the Janus Festival was used to highlight past events and prospects for newly hired staff who were beginning their employment in the New Year. See also Chapter 9 where I describe an interesting prop that was used in giving this presentation.
Arts & sciences honors students banquet	April 20: A momentous day for the arts: in 1896, Art nouveau was introduced at a Paris exhibition; for the humanities: birth in 121 A.C.E. of Marcus Aurelius, the Roman Emperor (161-180)—who authored *Meditations* among other works; for the sciences: in 1876—the founding in New York City of the American Chemical Society	Something of importance on this day happened relative to all fields of studies honored at this banquet

(continued)

Table 6.1. Use of Historic Events of the Day to Add Drama and Intrigue in Presentations *(continued)*

Presentation	*Date: Historical Event*	*Remarks or Context*
Faculty and staff retirement reception	May 17: Note that on this day important events occurred relative to the topics of separation, anxiety, and new beginnings. For separation: Norwegians honor their separation—in 1814—from Denmark; For anxiety: Inaugural use of the first merry-go-round—set up at a fair in Turkey in 1620; For new beginnings: Abraham Lincoln—nominated for the presidency in 1860	Mention how these historic events tie into three key characteristics of retirement and the experiences of professionals who are retiring, viz., Separation, Anxiety, and New Beginnings
Welcoming of families and prospective students at a university weekend orientation event	September 23: Noting that on this day important events occurred relative to the topics of fun, focus, and finish. For fun: in 1912, the Mack Sennett organization released the first Keystone Cops film comedy entitled, "Cohen Collects a Debt"; For focus: in 1986, following nearly 100 years of debate, the U.S. Congress an act declaring the "rose" as our country's national flower; and For finish: in 1806 Meriwether Lewis and William Clark returned to St Louis following their historic trip to the Western United States	I noted how these historic events tie into three key wishes university faculty members and administrative staff have for students; viz., that they have *Fun*, that they *Focus* on their studies, and that they *Finish* their programs and receive their degrees (Armstrong 2000)

Event honoring family members responsible for a bequest to the University of Arkansas for the renovation of an administrative conference room

November 8: Remarked how this day has been one of several new beginnings, including:

- In 1731, the first U.S. circulating library was established in the U.S.—by Benjamin Franklin—in his hometown of Philadelphia;
- In 1793, the Louvre opened in Paris;
- In 1889, Montana (Treasure State) was admitted as the 41st state of the Union;
- In 1932 Franklin Delano Roosevelt was elected President over his Republican and incumbent opponent, Herbert Hoover;
- In 1956, "The Ten Commandments"—the Cecil B. DeMille's epic—premiered in New York City;
- In 1960, John F. Kennedy defeated Richard Nixon in a close presidential race;
- In 1966, Ronald Reagan won his first term as governor of California defeating incumbent Edmund G. "Pat" Brown;
- In 1988, George Herbert Walker Bush elected President, defeating Massachusetts Governor Michael Dukakis

And, now at the University of Arkansas, we add to the list of important events of this day, the the naming and dedication of the Gus Lewis Conference Room relevance to topics in talks. For example, consider the bicentennial (2004-2006) of the Lewis and Clark expedition. This momentous anniversary can be used to point out its significance, not only to the opening of what would become a very large segment of the current Western United States (i.e., following the Louisiana Purchase of 1803; see *n. 1*) but also helping America establish, through President Thomas Jefferson's vision, the country's commitment to scholarly pursuits. By using this reference, you have the chance to remind audiences that it was Jefferson who instructed Meriwether Lewis and William Clark to not only survey and map the West but also to bring back information on geographical features, fauna and flora, and Native American languages and culture. Members of the so-called "Corps of Discovery" were also directed to send back flora and fauna specimens to Washington for study. The admonitions of Jefferson set an important pattern for learning in America (Duncan and Burns 1997).

In terms of education and learning, I have also alluded many times to the significant enhancement of America's higher education system through the actions of another great U.S. President, Abraham Lincoln. Indeed, it is a dramatic story to share that Lincoln, at the height of the U.S. Civil War and a time when the war was not going well for the Union (1862), took time to envision a brighter future and supported a bill that would provide college opportunities for the sons and daughters of the working class. The "power of Lincoln"—in the signing of the Morrill Act—set a course in the United States for the establishment of more than 75 great land-grant universities (e.g., Penn State, Michigan State, Iowa State, and Washington State Universities; the Universities of Arizona, Minnesota, and Wisconsin at Madison) (Williams 1991). Historic references, particularly those related to great presidents such as Jefferson and Lincoln, provide powerful anecdotes and stories that enhance the effectiveness of presentations.

Appendix 6 contains an array of historically interesting allusions and quotes by a variety of prominent figures including historians. Because of the enormity of possible references, the span of topics I have chosen is somewhat limited but I have shared many allusions and quotes that I have used effectively in presentations. I hope that some of these allusions and quotes might prove useful in talks that you give. Also, I hope that the examples given may spark ideas for other uses of historical allusions in presentations.

I would like to end this section with one of my favorite quotes about history and historians and it comes from Washington State University History Professor Jacqueline Peterson, who noted that "Historians can't quite be accused of inventing the past, but the craft of revivifying the dead is as much alchemy as science, inspired story telling as factual chronicle." So, think of history as a way of not only revivifying historic personages and past events but also helping to build drama and intrigue into presentations.

Just as historical anecdotes and stories provide powerful components for presentations, literary allusions offer extraordinary opportunities for heightening drama and intrigue.

LITERATURE

Perhaps akin to others, I recall vividly only a few lectures from my undergraduate days. But one lecturer and one presentation—in 1963 at that—stands out. The lecturer was Blaise Opulente (Professor of English at St. John's University in New York) and his message (to a group of pharmacy students) was this: "As an academic diagnostician I would like to prescribe three remedies as a possible corrective to the illnesses of excessive specialization, humanistic isolationism, an enfeebled emotional life, and spiritual starvation. These are: (1) continuing education; (2) the reading of seminal books; and (3) the development of an interdisciplinary attitude toward science." I have had many occasions to return to Professor Opulente's "prescriptions" and particularly his second admonition—which has become a touchstone for incorporation of literary allusions into talks and other presentations.

In parallel to the ideas about historical references, there is an enormous range and depth of literary material to draw from, but I'd like to share some thoughts about a few of my favorite allusions with specific references to their use in presentations about topics apart from the literary references per se. Thus, I hope to demonstrate by example how treasured literary works may be considered for use in presentations on topics near and dear to your professional life.

A few years ago, I was asked to make a presentation on the characteristics and future of graduate education. I developed a paper that was presented before several audiences including a group of faculty and graduate students at Far Eastern State University in Vladivostok, Russia. The paper's "literary links" were adopted from Lewis Carroll's Alice stories: *Alice's Adventures in Wonderland* and *Through the Looking Glass and What Alice Found There*—each with exquisite drawings by the famous *Punch* magazine illustrator, John Tenniel (see *n. 2*).

The Alice stories have been rich sources of allusions and metaphors for countless speakers. In the case of the graduate education presentations, the descriptions of several characteristics of graduate education were enhanced by juxtaposition of Carroll's thoughts and John Tenniel's wonderful drawings (see http://65.107.211.206/victorian/graphics/tenniel/alice/gallery1.html and http://65.107.211.206/victorian/graphics/tenniel/lookingglass/gallery4.html), captured in PowerPoint™ slides. For example, the occasional "madness" felt by the lonely graduate scholar is highlighted by the interchange between Alice and the Cheshire Cat: "'But I don't want to go around mad people,' Alice remarked. 'Oh, you can't help that,' said the Cat: 'we're all mad here. I'm mad. You're mad.' 'How do you know I'm mad?' said Alice. 'You must be,' said the Cat, 'or you wouldn't have come here.'" The allusions to occasionally apparent madness from focused study is not lost on audience members who have any familiarity with graduate study or other serious scholarship.

If you have wondered, by the way, where the expression "grin like a Cheshire-Cat" came from, it is apparently related to a common mid-nineteenth century practice of Cheshire cheese makers who prepared cheeses in the shape of a smiling cat's head (Gray 1992). Also, a once famous Cheshire sign painter from the same period was known to incorporate smiling cats into his works (Gray 1992).

Getting back to the graduate education presentation, the common experience of graduate students struggling to make progress in their research and scholarship was illustrated by Alice's interaction with the Red Queen. Remember when they were running in place? "'Now! Now!' cried the Queen. 'Faster! Faster!' And they went so fast that at last they seemed to skim through the air, hardly touching the ground with their feet, till suddenly, just as Alice was getting quite exhausted, they stopped, and she found herself sitting on the ground, breathless and giddy. The Queen propped her up against a tree, and said kindly, 'You may rest a little, now.' Alice looked round her in great surprise. 'Why, I do believe we've been under this tree the whole time! Everything's just as it was!' 'Of course it is,' said the Queen. 'What would you have it?' 'Well, in *our* country,' said Alice, still panting a little, 'you'd generally get to somewhere else—if you ran very fast for a long time as we've been doing.' 'A slow sort of country!' said the Queen. 'Now, *here*, you see, it takes all the running *you* can do, to keep in the same place. If you want to get somewhere else, you must run at least twice as fast as that!'" Certainly these expressions mirror the experiences of graduate students—particularly doctoral students at the time of the preparation of their dissertations.

Besides the use of quotes and drawings, I have found that Alice stories-embellished presentations are enlivened by a short historic prelude in which you may recount briefly the origins of these delightful tales (Clark 1979). Indeed, many people find it intriguing to learn that Lewis Carroll—a mathematics lecturer better known to his Oxford colleagues as Charles Lutwidge Dodgson—wrote the first Alice story following a fateful rendezvous with his Dean's daughter, Alice. The encounter occurred during a rowing adventure up the Isis river to Godstow in 1862.

The July 4th boat trip involved Lewis Carroll, his friend and fellow Oxford Don, Robinson Duckworth, and their Dean's three daughters: Alice Pleasance (age ten), Lorina (age thirteen), and Edith (age eight). During the afternoon's journey, Alice allegedly pleaded with Carroll, to "Tell us a story please." Carroll responded with a story modeled after Alice and began by having his heroine go, "straight down the rabbit-hole, to begin with, without the least idea what was to happen afterwards . . . " Hours later, the tale, in large measure, was told, and Alice would further plead, "Oh, I wish you would write down Alice's adventures for me." (Clark 1979).

Allegedly, Carroll began the writing process during the morning following the rowing trip. Eight months later, the manuscript for *Alice's Adventures Under Ground*, was complete. On November 26, 1864, Carroll gave a handwritten and personally illustrated version of the story to Alice Liddell (pronounced "liddle"), along with the dedication, "A Christmas Gift to a Dear Child in Memory of a Summer Day." This original manuscript is now housed in a glass case in the British Library and is available in facsimile version (Carroll 1986).

The historic interlude is inserted near the beginning of the presentation. The talk ends with the suggestion that if Alice were to return to the twenty-first century, she would—rather than going through the looking glass—dissolve through a computer screen.

Before going on to the use of popular culture references in talks, I'd like to briefly share just two other examples of how Opulente's "prescriptions" have been used to enrich presentations and interactions with different groups of people. The examples resulted from professional visits made to the University of Massachusetts at Amherst (UMass) and the University of Kansas.

The trip to UMass Amherst was pre-staged by reading about the life of Emily Dickinson—who, as many know, was a lifelong reclusive resident of Amherst. I also read more than two-hundred of her poems (Dickinson, 1996). Allusions to her life and poetry were woven throughout presentations given at the University. By coincidence, one of her poems so struck me that I chose it as a theme-setting verse for a presentation made during the launching of the University of Connecticut's research vessel—the *R/V Connecticut* in 1999, and here it is.

"Exultation is the going
Of an inland soul to sea,—
Past the houses, past the headlands,
Into deep eternity!

Bred as we, among the mountains.
Can the sailor understand
The divine intoxication
Of the first league out from land?"

The trip to the University of Kansas inspired some scholarly work that has since been used in many presentations.

Some scholars of *fin de siècle* literature believe that Lewis Carroll's "Alice," was a model for another little girl's adventure—Dorothy's trip to OZ. My visit to Kansas inspired me to read *The Wizard of OZ* (see *n. 3*).

Practically everyone is familiar with the 1939 classic OZ film starring Judy Garland (Dorothy), Ray Bolger (the farm hand Hunk and Scarecrow), Jack Haley (the farm hand Hickory and Tin Woodman), Bert Lahr (the farm hand Zeke and the Cowardly Lion), Frank Morgan (Professor Marvel, the OZ gate keeper, and the Wizard of OZ), Margaret Hamilton (the evil Kansas neighbor, Miss Gulch and the Wicked Witch of the West), and Billie Burke (Glinda the Good Witch of the North). However, I have found relatively few people (even during my trip to Kansas) who have read the original OZ book (Baum, 1900) or any of the dozens of follow-up volumes that were written and published after L. Frank Baum's original 1900 work with illustrations by W. W. Denslow (Baum and Hearn 2001; see also: http://www.geocities.com/Heartland/Meadows/6188/oz-authors.html). In fact, if you haven't read the book you may be surprised to learn of one of the important difference between the film and the book. While Dorothy's adventure was a dream in the film, in the book she really went to OZ. And, OZ took on geographical and cultural characteristics that became the platform for more than forty sequels that Baum and his successors wrote well into the second half of the twentieth century. Indeed, Baum himself wrote twelve sequels from 1900 to 1919, the year in which he died. Interestingly, the writer of the greatest number of OZ books was a woman: Ruth Plumy Thompson, which represents an interesting anecdote to share with audiences.

Some scholars believe that Dorothy represents the girl child that Baum never had. Thus, akin to Lewis Carroll, Baum wrote the *Wizard of OZ* for children near and dear to him; in Baum's case—his two sons and their young friends. But, like so many great tales written ostensibly for children, the OZ story has a message of great value, particularly for those of us who supervise personnel. Why? Because the OZ story embodies the theme of social leadership, which is centered about the value metaphors associated with the Scarecrow, the Tin Woodman, and the Cowardly Lion, namely, intelligence, kindness, and courage. Perhaps in an earlier time we would have said: faith, charity, and hope—in that order. I have used this allusion several times during staff recognition ceremonies and presentations to students and their parents—usually to the delight of all.

Before concluding this section, I would like to offer another tip that can be very helpful in engaging audiences in literary allusions used in talks. Akin to many readers and professional critics, I am fascinated by the origins of titles of books—particularly literary works. This fascination can be "tapped" by finding the lines in books or reviews that incorporate title words or references to the title—in intriguing or dramatic ways. You may also find—through reviews or other encounters, reasons for given titles. The reasons and their explication can heighten interest in literary allusions incorporated into presentations.

For example, when referring to Jane Austen's great masterpiece, *Pride and Prejudice*, I enjoy sharing a wonderful line in an "afterword" piece written by Joann Morse, "In a society devoted to surfaces and stereotypes it is no wonder that Elizabeth makes mistakes. [but] The story of their love affair is really the story of their progress in self-knowledge. They move beyond the roles fixed for them to become full human beings with insight and understanding, *rather than flat figures of pride and prejudice*." (italics added by me)

Having met in 1999 the Pulitzer Prize winning author of *Angela's Ashes*, Frank McCourt, I couldn't help asking him what was the reason behind the title? Was it the ashes from his mother's chain-smoked cigarettes? Was it the ashes of the fireplaces so critical to warmth in Limerick flats?

No! In his characteristically ironic manner, Frank noted that the title is somewhat of a misnomer, suggesting that he had intended initially that the book would cover a period embracing most of his and all of his mother's life. Thus, the ashes might be a metaphor for memories of his mom. As anyone who has read *Angela's Ashes* knows, both Frank and his mom are very much alive when the narrative of the book ends and the sequel, *'Tis* begins. But the "title story" adds color to references to McCourt's impressive works.

One final, though favorite, "title genesis" story is worth mentioning. The great W. Somerset Maugham novel, *The Razor's Edge*, derives its title from a verse in the Third Valli (chapter) of the *Katha Upanishad*, an ancient (1400–800 B.C.E.) Indian work. The verse translation used by Maugham, appears on a flyleaf of the original book as follows: "The sharp edge of a razor is difficult to pass over: thus the wise say the path to Salvation is hard."

But, you may—as I do—prefer another translation by F. Max Müller (1878–84):

"The sharp edge of a razor is difficult to pass over; thus the wise say the path (to the Self) is hard."

And, if you are familiar with the book and the wonderful Darryl F. Zanuck (Producer) and George Cukor (Director) film of the same name, starring Tyrone Power (as Larry Darrell), Jean Tierney (as Isabel) and Clifton Webb (as Elliott), you love the story of a man (Larry) who searches for the meaning of life—through interdisciplinary study and travel while having relationships with people whose values are superficial (Isabel, Elliott et al.). Thus, the "title genesis," the story, and its connections to the marvelously cast film add life to a great theme worthy of allusion in presentations.

So, be cognizant of title references in books and reviews that offer literary allusions for speeches and other presentations. The references will help you enhance drama and intrigue in your talks.

Concluding this section on literature, I recommend Opulente's cogent advice—with a twist. Speaking and other professional tasks can be enriched immensely by integrating self-directed continuing education with allusions to selected readings, a few of which I have shared in this section. I also wish to share other favorite allusions and quotes from a variety of literary sources and these are contained in Appendix 7. Parallel to the discussion on history, my list is hardly exhaustive, but I have tried to share personal favorites. With this sharing, I also hope that you may think about Opulente's "prescriptions" during your reading for pleasure. Take notes. Compile reference material. Develop and begin building up an inventory of allusions that may be used—metaphorically, figuratively, or literally—in future presentations.

History and literature are rich sources of materials for talks, but these sources can be further enriched by allusions to popular culture.

POPULAR CULTURE

Under the rubric of "popular culture," I include music, television shows and films, games, and ephemeral objects typically associated with fads. The latter will be addressed in a subsequent portion of Section II under Artifacts and Props. For now, let's consider principally how allusions to music, television shows and films, and games may be incorporated into talks to instill drama and intrigue.

Song titles and lyrics—referred to properly and used sparingly under fair-use provisions of U.S. copyright law (see Appendix 8)—prompt special recognition and provide intriguing approaches to analogies and symbolism in presentations. For example, I referenced the 1940's song, "There Will Never be Another You" (Mack Gordon, lyrics and Harry Warren, music) in the Bob Gray eulogy (noted earlier) in conjunction with my reference to him being "one-in-a-billion."

Frank Broyles, legendary sports announcer and University of Arkansas Athletic Director (popularly referred to as "Coach") who has been employed into his late seventies (in 2003), likes to refer to the Elton John song, "I'm Still Standing," in comments about the "Coach's" longevity.

The line, "Where have you gone Joe DiMaggio?" from the Paul Simon and Art Garfunkel song, "Mrs. Robinson," has served as one-half of a hyphenated title to a research ethics talk that I have given before numerous academic groups. The title and a few other lines of the song—help to draw the audience into a talk that requires discussion of several dark elements of human behavior. For example, I will ask the audience to recall the song's lines: "We'd like to know a little bit about you for our files . . .", "We'd like to help you learn to help yourself . . .", and "Hiding in a hiding place where no one ever goes . . .", which help to set the mood for some of the sober research ethics topics to follow.

I have also used the title and a few lines of the Jim Croce song "Time in a Bottle," to craft talks used as a personal farewell or to welcome new staff at orientations and related social events. Let me elaborate a bit more.

Both presentations are begun with the admission of not being a great fan of popular music of the sixties and seventies but akin to the rediscovery of the works of Bach (1685–1750) through the advocacy of Felix Mendelssohn (1809–1847) in the nineteenth century, I have been re-discovering in later life what many believe to be important contributions during these musically influential decades—including among them, the works of Jim Croce. Following a poignant reminder to audiences of the untimely death of Croce at thirty-two year's old (d. airplane accident in Natchitoches [pronounced by Louisianans as "Nak-a-dish"], LA—September 20, 1973), I point out that my favorite work of his is "Time in a Bottle." After which, I begin reading—but end—singing the last few lines of the first two stanzas of this haunting song, which you will recall contains the elements of: (1) posing if we could save time in a bottle, (2) we would like to spend eternity with the ones we love (in stanza 1); and, (3) there never seems to be enough time to be with our loved ones and (4) who are the ones we want to spend our lives with (stanza 2). The actual lyrics, which may be adoptable under fair use provisions (Section 107; see also Appendix 8) of the 1976 U.S. Copyright Act, are very powerful in their effects on audiences.

To complete the context for the use of the "Time in a Bottle" song, let me elaborate a bit more on the remaining portions of the two related presentations.

I view the "time in a bottle" metaphor as an extension of a common childhood fantasy about putting a message in a bottle and casting it into the ocean with the hope that some unsuspecting beachcomber in a far-off land will find it, relish the shared thoughts, and contact you. One can note at this juncture in the presentations that two women—in their teens—did cast a message-bearing bottle into Long Island Sound in 1979. The bottle was subsequently retrieved along the Irish Coast in 2000!

After sharing the Croce lines and the note-in-a-bottle anecdote, the message of the talk takes one of two tacks, depending on whether it is a personal farewell or welcoming presentation to others. In the former, I share a fantasy about a mythical bottle that follows me around—via the Iowa River, the Colorado River (Texas), the Snake River (Washington and Idaho), the Connecticut River, and now the Arkansas River—rivers in close proximity to universities where I have worked during the past thirty-five years. The talk is completed with the suggestion that when my days are through I hope that a friendly river god will give the bottle to a survivor—hopefully—my wife. In it she will find three messages: 1) "You never know!"; 2) "He loved his wife Marsha June with all of his heart."; 3) "He tried to serve—well—all the institutions where he worked and lived out his personal and professional drama." These messages and the conclusion of the talk are usually received with tears among family and friends.

In the case of the welcoming permutation of the "time in a bottle" talk, the speaking-singing message is followed by allusions to the advice of Thoreau (1854), Peck (1978), Buscaglia (1982), and many other sages—that life is not all goals and accomplishments but "getting there" (see also Appendix 3). For new employees, the gentle cajoling is that it is important to treasure moments with colleagues, students, and friends during their years at the institution—to save as it were their "time in a bottle"—in order to savor these memories in the years ahead. This conclusion—like the one in the farewell speech—is received with appreciation and joy.

I have used one other song and composer story in welcoming addresses for new staff. The song comes from *West Side Story*, and begins with the singing of two stanzas of "Something's Coming," which begins with "Could be, who knows?" and continues with the thoughts: (1) something great may be coming, (2) something bright and wonderful (in stanza 1); and, (3) something great maybe near or just about to happen to me, (4) if I can wait, it "is gonna be great" (stanza 2). The actual lyrics, which may be adoptable under fair use provisions (Section 107; see also Appendix 8) of the 1976 U.S. Copyright Act, are poignant.

The talk continues with the question: Do you remember? Then, "Sure you do. It's one of Tony's songs from *West Side Story* which opened on Broadway on September 27, 1957." I go on to suggest that most people remember the music of *West Side Story* being written by Leonard Bernstein. But, fewer people know about the play's song lyrics, which were composed by a twenty-seven year old Stephen Sondheim (Brantley 2001). And, herein lies the "hook" for newcomers, or more specifically their new careers in your organization. At this point, I suggest a title for my presentation: "Something's Coming—Possibly the Rest of Your Career." I also suggest that there are parallels among Sondheim's life, newcomers' careers, and the mission and raison d'etre of the organization they are now serving (in my case, a university).

As background, a bit of history is in order, relative to Sondheim's life (McCabe 2002). You can mention that following his parents' divorce, Sondheim, then in his mid-teens, moved with his mom from New York City to Doylestown, Pennsylvania, where they happened to locate close to Oscar Hammerstein. The year was 1945 and around the time Hammerstein was beginning his fateful set of collaborations with Richard Rodgers.

The story continues with allusions to how Hammerstein began a mentoring relationship with Sondheim—wherein the former became a father figure as well. The relationship, in turn, had a profound effect on Sondheim, who would remark in latter life "I would have become a geologist if Oscar had been a geologist." (McCabe 2002). But, of course, Sondheim, under the tutelage of Hammerstein would become a brilliant lyricist—one not known necessarily for "blockbuster hits" but one who accumulated a series of memorable contributions including, *A Funny Thing Happened on the Way to the Forum*, *Gypsy*, *Into the Woods*, *Sunday in the Park With George*, and of course, *West Side Story*.

As my presentation continues, I suggest that parallel bodies of work are what my faculty colleagues might look to achieve while they are at the university. And, the mentoring experienced by Sondheim presents a wonderful model for the teaching relationships we wish our new faculty members to have with students. These messages are received well, but the drama and intrigue of the presentation is heightened greatly by the initial singing of a few lines of the memorable Bernstein/Sondheim song.

Now, if you are really brave, you might take the use of songs in presentations—just one step further. Consider a group sing that could be used as a prelude to a short presentation. For example, during a recent winter holiday season at the University of Arkansas, I organized a group consisting of the Chairman of our University Faculty Senate (who happens to be a great baritone singer), his wife and mine, and a music student who provided piano accompaniment. After a few preliminary remarks, we led the assembly of about one-hundred and fifty people in the singing of the marvelous song, "The Twelve Days of Christmas." You may remember the elements: partridge in a pear tree, two turtle doves, three French hens, four calling birds, five gold rings, six geese a-laying, seven swans a-swimming, eight maids a-milking, nine ladies dancing, ten lords a-leaping, eleven pipers piping, and twelve drummers drumming. The performance was embellished by a necktie I wore containing representations of the elements and characters in the song and having one of my singing partners point to each of these elements successively as we worked through the stanzas of the song.

With the singing over, I thanked my fellow performers, and proceeded to offer some background and insight to the song. Point-wise, the monolog can be crafted something like this:

- The twelve days of Christmas occur between Christmas day (December 25) and the Epiphany or Little Christmas on January 6 (a day of Christmas celebrations in many parts of the world).

- Contrary to several modern myths that the twelve-day legend and song are attributable to sacred symbols and beliefs, including persecuted English Catholics' (1558-1829) attempts to link faith-based beliefs to secular themes, the rhyming words and song have their roots in eighteenth century France, where they may have been used as word-games.
- The twelve-day words were first published in England in 1780—in a children's book *Mirth Without Mischief*.
- The common interpretations of the days' meanings are generally correct except that the "four calling birds" were probably "four colly birds" (black birds; remember the four and twenty black birds baked in a pie?).
- The five gold rings, rather than being representative of jewelry—as is commonly portrayed in modern-day works—were probably references to the five gold rings about the necks of pheasants.
- Thus, the first seven days are about food; the eighth (eight maids a-milking) —about sauces; and, the ninth through the twelfth days—merriment.
- How marvelous!
- How French!!
- The Twelve Days of Christmas is all about food and merriment!!!
- Or, as we might imagine Lucy from Charles Schultz's "Peanuts" saying: "All about parties, and handsome boys and *pretty* girls."

The song skit and presentation ends with greetings and good wishes for all. And, great joy!

There are undoubtedly many other songs and sets of lyrics that can be alluded to or blended—through song—into talks. And, if you combine singing with poignant lyrics you can create memorable interludes for presentations of various types.

If I made my song-enhanced presentations in Ireland, audiences probably would not be so surprised by singing during a public presentation. But, in the U.S. at least, it turns out to be quite a dramatic gesture—one that is received with delight—even coming from yours truly who is clearly not in the league of the "three tenors." If you adopt such a tactic, you may—as I have—find people coming up to you months later with the line, "It was fun to have you sing to our group!"

In addition to musical lyrics and songs, television shows and films offer interesting tools and materials for talks.

Chere Campbell Gibson of the University of Wisconsin-Madison is known (Gibson 2002) to begin talks with three hypothetical answers to a theme question—in the style of the popular TV quiz show—*Jeopardy*. In a recent presentation, this approach was played out in terms of distance education. Thus, she started her presentation with the statements: "The train has left the station," "It's the thing to do," and "It will secure the bottom line of our University"—as answers to the question: "Should we be adding distance education to the panoply of programs at our university"?—a key question relevant to the remainder of her presentation.

Gibson's television-show technique is an engaging and thoughtful approach to a talk's beginning. One can imagine parallel uses of game show formats (e.g., the multiple choice question format of "Who wants to be a millionaire?" and other similar shows) to enhance drama and intrigue in talks, including exciting conclusions.

Regarding conclusions to talks, I have used allusions to a popular fifties television show to engage audiences and make points about the role of research universities in economic development. Some background is in order.

Through the work of the University of Arkansas (92 to 100-member) 2010 Commission, a ten-year plan was crafted to guide development of the University based on the premise that university efforts in teaching, research, and service have powerful impacts on the economic, cultural, and intellectual lives of the state's citizens. The *Making the Case* plan (2001) features return-on-investment information for higher education in general and research in particular. Returns to the State's economy of seven-to-twenty-three percent compounded yearly were determined with direct payoffs in terms of new state revenues from enhanced employment of university graduates, new jobs, and intellectual property to spur high technology industrial development. To emphasize these points and as an ending to presentations on the 2010 Commission's plan, I play a little game with audiences using allusions to high density electronics on the one hand and the *Howdy Doody Show* of early television history—on the other.

My game begins with a slide containing representations of modern high-density television flat screens of today and a TV set from the early fifties. I initially make points about how university-based research has contributed to improved reliability and image clarity of modern television sets. Audience members are then challenged to think about the unreliability and fuzzy images common with vintage televisions. After setting these images in the minds of audience members, I ask them to close their eyes for 30 seconds and think about the first time they viewed television programming.

After opening their eyes, I relate my first experience—and here I admit my age—in 1948 when I watched daily in Queens, New York, the *Howdy Doody Show* (first broadcast on December 27, 1947). I then reminisce a bit about how NBC in the late forties did not come on the air in New York until 5:30 in the afternoon and how the signal was pre-staged by a test pattern with a picture of the head of puppet extraordinaire—Howdy Doody—a creation of Buffalo Bob Smith (formerly Schmidt). I then turn to a slide with pictures of characters from Doodyville and pose to the audience the challenge that I will give a golden-colored Sacagewea dollar to anyone who can name the likes of Dilly Dally, Phinerly T. Bluster, Clarabell, and the Flub-a-dub. There usually aren't that many people in the audience who can do the naming but enough to make the game interesting. At end, I comment about Sacagawea and her critical role in the Lewis and Clark Expedition, alluding to the President Jefferson story I related in an earlier part of this book. I have used the Howdy Doody routine during several service club presentations and it has been a hit every time.

Akin to television shows, allusions to films, and use of selected clips can add much to presentations. Leroy Ashby, national award winning history professor at Washington State University, has been using multi-media in history presentations well before the word "multi-media" was coined. His talks on twentieth century American history have been legendarily enriched by film and audio clips.

In presentations where allusions to the *Wizard of OZ* story are highlighted, I have shown a short clip from the Academy Award winning 1939 film to set the stage for the question, "How many of you have seen this film?" The question usually gets a near unanimous yes-response. Then, I follow with: "Now, how many have read the nineteen hundred L. Frank Baum book?" Far fewer people typically raise their hands. You can then provide a little historical context before launching into the leadership model imbedded in the story—as noted earlier.

I have also used the characters in the *Wizard of OZ* film to craft a concluding game in talks related to leadership. In this case, the game revolves around the question, "which actors played the Scarecrow, the Tin Woodman, the Cowardly Lion and others in the film?" Additionally, questions can be added about the multiple roles played by Ray Bolger, Jack Haley, Bert Lahr, Frank Morgan, and Margaret Hamilton (as noted earlier).

Still shots from films—used selectively and sparingly in the context of fair use provisions (Section 107; see also Appendix 8) of the 1976 U.S. Copyright Act, As Amended can also be incorporated effectively in talks. For example, I have used a still shot of the monster from the 1931 classic, *Frankenstein*, portrayed brilliantly by Boris Karloff. The still shot is a part of a historic introduction to a talk I have given many times on the topic of human subjects research. While projecting the still shot, I tell the story of Mary Wollstonecraft Shelley's novel (1818) of the same name, wherein the scientist was Frankenstein, the monster nameless. Audiences are fascinated to learn that the novel was written as a result of a contest among Mary Wollstonecraft Shelley, the poet Percy Bysshe Shelley, Lord (George Gordon) Byron, and his secretary Polidari during a rainy summer holiday in Switzerland (see *n. 4*). Of course, Mary Wollstonecraft Shelley was the winner and the subsequently published book became a best seller. My talk continues with a recitation of the admonishment from the nineteenth century classic, "If the study to which you apply yourself has a tendency to weaken you affections, and to destroy your taste for those simple pleasures in which no alloy can possibly live, then that study is certainly unlawful, that is to say, not befitting the human mind."—as a prelude to a discussion of nineteenth century values that shaped future thinking about the use of human subjects in research.

There is one further technique I would like to relate about the use of popular culture in talks. This technique has literary roots and relies on a reference to a well-known series of children's books.

Audiences containing people from the last two to three generations of the twentieth century relate favorably to references to the "Gold Bug" found in Richard Scarry's books (see example cited in Bibliography). Many recall as a parent, grand-parent or child reading these complexly illustrated books with the enjoyable exercise of finding the small character known as the "Gold Bug," among the various anthropomorphized creatures that appear on most pages of Scarry's works.

The use of the "gold bug" works this way. Following some remarks to remind audience members of this charming feature of Scarry's works, you suggest that "gold bugs" have been placed in slides of your presentation—to tweak interest and to use—possibly as a basis for rewards. Let me offer a concrete example.

During a recent year, I was asked to speak in a music appreciation class at the University of Arkansas. The instructor of the course had heard my "future of the University" talk at another venue and wanted the more than seven hundred first-year students distributed among three sections of his course to hear that message.

Because of the nature of the course, I thought that I should combine purposes. Thus, the "gold bugs" were actually pictures of famous composers and performers. Single pictures were inserted in varying places in about two-thirds of the PowerPoint™ slides. The pictures included portrayals of Count Basie, Ludwig von Beethoven, Chuck Berry, Madonna, Wolfgang Amadeus Mozart, and Willie Nelson, among others. As I came to each slide—with a pictured musical great—I asked if there were members of the class who could identify the "gold bug." If they thought they could, I then asked them to name the music personality and to say something meaningful about the personage or their work.

If correct answers were offered, I gave each of the students a 3 × 5 in. index card with a gold star in the corner. With the prior permission of the instructor, students with correct answers were asked to write their answers on the card and turn them into the instructor for extra credit.

The "gold bug" talk was a great hit with the students—young and old. You can undoubtedly imagine a variety of approaches—musically oriented or not—for using the "gold bug" technique. I think you'll find that it provides an entrée to enhanced drama and intrigue in your presentations.

Besides the specific examples noted above, one might imagine the selected and limited use of still shots from famous films such as *Star Wars*, *Star Trek*, *Harry Potter*, and the *Lord of the Rings* to illustrate allusions to heroic imagery that provides rich material for inspirational presentations.

You are only limited by your imagination relative to allusions to television shows and films that may be woven into talks. But, from the examples offered above, it should be clear that such allusions may add significantly to the drama and intrigue of presentations.

Besides references to television game shows, there is, of course, the realm of board games that also provide a rich source of references and bases for metaphors. I have also coupled board game allusions with references to a popular movie to make dramatic and intriguing points about games and goals in life.

Recently, I have been using board game allusions in talks on professional and personal development. The talk begins with a reminder that there are three most common types of board games, which can be somewhat prosaically referred to as "clearing-the-board," "rearranging the board," and "filling-the-board" games.

The talk continues with the suggestion that practically everyone has had a chance to play different types of board games, but just for the record, I ask the audience to consider the games a bit more and specifically in the context of the theme of the talk.

"Clearing-the-board" games include *Checkers* (also known as Draughts), *Chess* (the "royal game"), and a chess-relative *Kriegspiel* (a "wargame" of German origin that is played by two individuals who make moves on separate boards while they are shielded from one another and where the moves are announced by a referee who sees both boards simultaneously). In terms of personal and professional development, we can think of "clearing-the-board" games as metaphors for times when it is advantageous to "clear" obstacles or other impediments from our lives.

"Rearranging-the-board" games are exemplified by *Chinese Checkers*, *Chutes and Ladder*s, and *Parcheesi*. Considering personal and professional development, the "rearranging-the-board" game may be thought of as a metaphor for reconfiguring one's talents and skills or what is commonly referred to as "reinventing oneself."

"Filling-the-board" games are exemplified by *Scrabble*®, the ancient Chinese game of *Go*—now very popular in Japan and other Asian countries, and a game co-developed in the United States by John Forbes Nash (remember the Oscar-winning film *A Beautiful Mind*)—a game called *Hex*, which he apparently played with great skill (Nasar 1994).

The remainder of the talk centers around the notion that life and indeed the remaining years of the lives of professionals can most effectively be compared to "filling-the-board" games such as *Hex*, which is played using a rhombus (equilateral parallelogram)-shaped board molded with contiguous hexagon shaped wells and two opposing black and two opposing white sides. Two people play the game as in *Chess*, but the purpose of the game is to fill the board—as necessary—in alternating sequence of play—with hexagon-shaped black or white pieces in a continuous line of single colored pieces while preventing your opponent from doing the same. The game is therefore similar to the ancient game of *Go* but instead of capturing territory—in *Hex*—you attempt to craft continuous, though possibly circuitous lines from one side of the board to another.

As the game proceeds—and as you can imagine because of blocking moves by your opponent—the *Hex* board typically fills up to a great extent; and, the victor is the one who can not only think strategically but one who has a keen sense of pattern recognition. Here's where the metaphor for lifetime goals comes in.

The audience is asked to imagine their life's history as a *Hex* board—with their filling in spaces as they learn and grow in wisdom. I then suggest—extending the metaphor a bit further—that we should all continually be looking for patterns and interconnected understanding with maturity and growth. This advice dovetails with our modern understanding of the highly interdisciplinary and interconnected world of the twenty-first Century and my belief that the most successful professionals and the most fulfilled human beings will be those who constantly fill in and connect meaningfully the intellectual, emotional, and social components of their lives. These allusions allow me to once again recommend Opulente's prescriptions ("(1) continuing education, (2) the reading of seminal books, and (3) the development of an interdisciplinary attitude toward science") with the specific goal of "filling in the game board of life" in especially attractive and meaningful ways.

One may enhance the ending of "board-game talks" through the use of a prop. Adopting a strategy akin to that noted in Chapter 5 for works of art, an easel can be located near the area from which you are giving your speech. The object—a *Scrabble® Board*—can be cloaked with an opaque cloth, which is removed ceremoniously at talk's end to reveal a series of *Scrabble®* ties pasted onto the board to spell-out a meaningful message to audience members, which may then be read aloud.

I used the board-game talk as a commencement speech in 2002 (see figure 6.1) and during a subsequent part of the ceremony in which graduates came across stage to receive their diplomas, several took the moment—while I shook their hands—to note "great speech." These signs of respect signaled the drama and intrigue that was obviously felt and appreciated by student members of the audience.

For the more sober minded, it may be thought that I have gone from the sublime to the ridiculous, in the transition from history and literature to popular culture. Well, if you are of that ilk, take heart, because we are now going to shift to a more serious topic—science and technology and their usefulness in building drama and intrigue into talks.

Fig. 6.1. Use of a *Scrabble Board*® to send a parting message to an audience; photo by Russell A. Cothren (SCRABBLE is a trademark of Hasbro in the U.S. and Canada and is used with permission. © 2003 Hasbro, Inc. All Rights Reserved.)

NOTES

1. Duncan, Dayton and Ken Burns, *The Journey of the Corps of Discovery—Lewis & Clark*, Knopf, New York, 1997; the Louisiana Purchase included all or part (p) of the following current-day states: Arkansas, Colorado (p), Idaho (p), Iowa, Kansas, Louisiana (p), Minnesota (p), Missouri, Montana (p), Nebraska, New Mexico (p), North Dakota (p), Oklahoma, South Dakota (p), Texas (p), and Wyoming (p).

2. Carroll, Lewis, *Alice's Adventures in Wonderland*, (originally published in 1865) and *Through the Looking Glass and What Alice Found There* (originally published in 1872) with drawings by John Tenniel, Penguin, New York, 1960; one can also read the original manuscript crafted by Carroll (including his own drawings) and given to Alice Liddell on November 26, 1864; available in a facsimile version: Lewis Carroll, *Alice's Adventures Under Ground*, with a forward by Mary Jean St Clair (Alice Liddell's granddaughter), Pavilion, London, 1985.

3. Baum, Lyman Frank, *The Wizard of OZ*, Puffin Books, New York, 1982; originally published in 1900 by George M. Hill Co. (Chicago) as *The Wonderful Wizard of OZ* and illustrated by W. (William) W. (Wallace) Denslow; reissued in 1903 by Bobbs-Merrill Co. (Indianapolis) as *The New Wizard of OZ*, and subsequently reprinted simply as *The Wizard of OZ*.

4. The crafting of the *Frankenstein* story by Mary Wollstonecraft Shelley is described nicely in the Introduction of the book's edition referenced in the Bibliography.

Chapter Seven

Science and Technology

It may not seem so from your reading to this point, but science and technology-related efforts have been at the heart of much of my career—including hundreds of presentations—long and short. Accordingly, I am comfortable discussing science- and technology-based topics. But, even for individuals whose lives include careers in areas such as business, the law, media or social services, allusions to science and technology can be developed and incorporated—effectively—into myriad talks. Indeed, I have been impressed with the capacity of people whose education has been primarily in the humanities and social sciences—to grasp and portray science and technology. Capable reporters, lobbyists and legislative staffers, among others, have shaped my positive impressions. These experiences should give you courage to take on the description of scientific and technological advances to a variety of groups, including audiences composed of people who are not well-versed in science and technology.

What I have found in making science and technology-based presentations is that audiences greatly appreciate your ability to bring clarity and insightful understanding to a topic that may have seemed arcane—previously. The effort requires a minimization of jargon, simple definitions, and the liberal use of analogy to objects and processes commonly understood by general audience members. For example, the parallels drawn among letters, words, sentences, paragraphs, and books to the bases, codons, genes, chromosomes, and genomes, respectively, of plants and animals, are commonly used as analogies to help explain the organization and function of DNA.

So, take on science and technology allusions in talks, but be careful of clarity and understanding. Consider testing your explanations on friends and relatives (including those with solid backgrounds in science and technology), remembering the words of Beveridge (1957), "In explaining a problem to another person, and especially to someone not familiar with that field of science, it is necessary to clarify and amplify aspects of it that have been taken for granted . . . Not infrequently it happens that while one is making the explanation, a new thought occurs to one without the other person having said a word."

Interest in scientific and technological materials is heightened when advances in these fields can be related to the specific interests of audience members. A group of primary and secondary school teachers, for example, may be very interested in understanding you may be able to offer about the neurological mechanisms of attention-enhancing drugs (e.g., methylphenidate or Ritalin™). Similarly, taxpayer groups concerned with the expenditure of U.S. tobacco court settlement funds may be more interested in genomic (genetics) and proteomic (study of proteins produced by genes) research if it can be connected with DNA-coded proteins that are involved in cancer and cardiovascular diseases.

Besides biomedical investigations, research related to space and environmental sciences spark considerable general interest. Audiences are intrigued by results of explorations that help us understand the origins and size of the universe. I am particularly fond of allusions to space probes such as the Pioneer 10 spacecraft which was launched in 1972, carried out its exploratory mission, and then went on to became the first human-made object to leave the solar system on June 13, 1983.

You may also like to consider a reference to the National Aeronautics and Space Administration (NASA) Genesis project which has placed a collector probe at a point between the sun and earth where gravity is equi-balanced (Lagrangian point, L1) for the purpose of collecting solar wind particles, which when retrieved, will help us understand the nature of particles formed about the time of the "big-bang"—more than 10 billion years ago.

Information on the Pioneer, Genesis, and other fascinating missions can be obtained through the NASA website (http://www.nasa.gov/) and that of the National Air and Space Museum (http://www.nasm.edu/).

Advances in environmental sciences—especially research that leads to cleaner energy sources or environmental cleanup processes are of great interest to the public. For example, when I lived in the northwestern United States, I was able to enrich many a talk with allusions to the challenges faced with the cleanup of the Hanford Reservation and its remnants of plutonium research and production during the later years of World War II and most years of the Cold War. Particularly exciting were research efforts that are leading to the solidification of contaminated soils into glasses suitable for long-term storage.

Efforts by the Pacific Northwest National Laboratories and its affiliated contractors on alternative energy sources such as solar cells, were also common components of talks given during my "Northwest days."

Information on environmental studies can be found on the websites of the Environmental Protection Agency (http://www.epa.gov/), the U.S. Department of Energy (http://www.energy.gov/), and non-profit environmental organizations such as the National Council for Science and the Environment (http://www.cnie.org/).

I'll have more to share about the crafting of science and technology presentations in Section III, but allusions to these critical aspects of modern civilization represent important adjuncts to talks of various types. And, interest in science and technology will be enhanced when the material is connected with your audience. The connections may be social, economic, or merely pride of affiliation (e.g., presentations to alumni groups regarding results of research conducted at their alma maters), but associations of science and technology with the lives of audience members or people they know (e.g., health-related research and sick relatives) can provide powerful benefits in presentations. Indeed, such connections or linkages also involve the social sciences, which are considered next.

Chapter Eight

Social Sciences

Akin to the topics of history, literature, science, and technology, we take on a broad span of learning when considering the social sciences. Embracing as they do, economics, political science, psychology, and sociology, not to mention derivative fields such as criminal justice, public policy, and social work, there is much to draw upon. Fortunately, for the non-expert, the social sciences, and for that matter the sciences and technology have become more interdisciplinary in recent decades thereby making more accessible the fruits of scholarly work in all related fields.

Because people are innately attracted to an understanding of self—individually and collectively, allusions embodying results of social sciences research are inherently interesting. More specifically, you will find allusions to the following topic areas of great interest to general audiences:

- Results of scientific polling that illuminate social attitudes and conditions
- Social psychology, especially that which illuminates altruistic or abhorrent behavior
- The brain-mind nexus
- Economic conditions and forecasting
- Political dynamics and the evaluation of public leaders
- Testing of cognitive skills
- Competition and sports psychology

Let's delve a bit more into each of these topics and their associated tools and materials.

POLLING AND SOCIAL ATTITUDES AND CONDITIONS

Polling often gets a bad rap for being overemphasized in its influence on political leaders. However, Everett Ladd, long-time director of the Roper Center at the University of Connecticut, was fond of noting that modern scientific polling was helping the United States evolve from a pure representative democracy to a hybrid of a participatory and representative democracy—a hybrid that would have intrigued the country's founders. Beyond its influence on politics, polling results provide insights on social attitudes and behaviors that audiences find intriguing.

For example, who in America would not be interested in the results of the U. S. pre-World War II polling question: If you had no choice but to live under a communistic or fascist form of government, which would you choose? The polling results—conducted through the infant Roper organization in 1937—indicated 67% fascist and 33% communistic. I have shared that result with numerous audiences—always with great resulting intrigue.

The results of scientific polling are available through a variety of archives and services including the Gallup Organization (http://www.gallup.com/), the Inter-University Consortium for Political and Social Research (http://www.icpsr.umich.edu/index.html), the Henry J. Kaiser Foundation, Public Opinion and Medical Research Service with links to various public opinion polling resources (e.g., Louis Harris and Associates, NBC News) (http://www.kaisernetwork.org/index.cfm), the Pew Research Center (http://www.people-press.org/), and the Roper Center for Public Opinion Research at the University of Connecticut (http://www.ropercenter.uconn.edu/). The trick is to craft a question that may have been asked in the time frame relevant to your presentation and weave the results into the talk in a dramatic or intriguing manner.

For example, a talk alluded to earlier on the use of tobacco settlement funds to support research related to tobacco-induced diseases, will be illuminated not only by figures on the percentage of smokers among the U.S. population but also stated desires of current smokers to quit.

There are many questions such as these that can be addressed through polling results. Your audiences will appreciate the references.

SOCIAL PSYCHOLOGY AND BEHAVIOR

Attitudes and social conditions that reflect the action of individuals—their motivations and behavior—especially that which is altruistic or aberrant—is of great interest to audiences. Thus, I rarely refer to a person in a talk without saying something about the apparent social psychological antecedents of their efforts.

Having met Frank McCourt (the author of *Angela's Ashes* [1996] and *'Tis* [1999]) a few years ago, I revel in sharing his view of emerging fame as being analogous to first wading into cold surf, feeling the waves strike higher and higher on your body and thinking "Oh! Oh!" But, who could mention Frank McCourt without referring to the destitute conditions of his childhood in Limerick, Ireland? How could you not appreciate his struggles as an adolescent immigrant (i.e., including the alleged molestation by a Catholic priest) in New York (McCourt 1999) without thinking about the social psychological effects of such a childhood experience?

The enthusiasm that the American public displays in biography as a genre for books, magazines, and films, reflects a strong interest in social psychology and bespeaks of the power of such reference material in presentations.

BRAIN-MIND NEXUS

Psychology, as a field of study, has its roots in the late nineteenth century. Through much of the twentieth century, however, the issue of the brain-mind nexus was a blur. If you read psychology textbooks from the middle and even latter part of the twentieth century, descriptions of the mind seem almost devoid of references to the physical brain. Enter the areas of study variously referred to as experimental or physiological psychology, cognitive science, and neuroscience, which have helped illuminate extraordinary relationships among brain anatomy, chemistry, and physiology, and function and behavior—relationships that are of great interest to audiences.

Who could, for example, tackle the talk alluded to earlier about the use of psycho stimulants in treating attention deficit disorders without touching upon the neurochemical correlates of such drug use?

ECONOMICS AND FORECASTING

Even among economists, the field of economics is referred to as the "dismal science." But, economists have one of the hardest jobs of all—ferreting out relationships and trends from systems fraught with variables that they—least of all—have any control of. As imprecise a study as it may seem at times, economics is still a vital science and one that is of interest to audiences particularly as it relates to economic forecasting.

As noted earlier, talks and references therein to the future are intriguing to most people. Indeed, as Kettering noted, "We are interested in the future because it is where we will spend the rest of our lives." Accordingly, projections of future economic growth and its relationship to the affiliations of audience members will be of great interest. Other facets of the economy such as job growth and unemployment rates may be of interest and data of this type—for the United States—can be obtained through the U.S. Department of Commerce (http://home.doc.gov/).

POLITICAL DYNAMICS AND POLITICAL LEADERSHIP

If anyone doubts audience intrigue in political dynamism and leadership, they need only be reminded of the ambiguities and vote-counting challenges the United States experienced during the extended process that led to the election of George W. Bush as President in 2000. The workings of political processes and the evaluation of leadership are of great interest to large segments of society.

Living in Northwest Arkansas in recent years has afforded the benefit of attending—once monthly—meetings of a loosely knit organization known as Political Animals. The group convenes at 7:00 A.M. on weekdays and turnouts in excess of one-hundred people are common for a presentation by a current or past politico or columnist. Following the presentation, the question and answer period typically extends beyond the time allotted.

Northwest Arkansas is certainly not a microcosm of the United States, but the popularity of the Political Animals group does testify to the great interest many people—particularly those who have a heightened social consciousness—have in politics and political processes. By incorporating relevant comments in your talks you will heighten intrigue so long as you avoid "showing your political stripes."

TESTING OF COGNITIVE SKILLS

People in the United States have great interest in the testing of cognitive skills. Perhaps because of the increasing importance being placed on testing and the advancement of pupils in elementary and secondary schools, as well as entrance of candidates into undergraduate (e.g., ACT and SAT exams) and graduate programs (e.g., GRE, GMAT exams), you will hardly find an audience that hasn't had some experience with testing activities. Accordingly, references to standardized examinations—their apparent benefits and pitfalls—will always spark interest particularly if you are in a position to comment on the relative importance of these measures either as an educator or private sector employer.

University and alumni group audiences, for example, are generally interested in average standardized scores for students admitted to their institutions *versus* national means. When such data can be coupled with information on national rankings (e.g., *U.S. News & World Report*, *Princeton Review*, *Fiske Guide to Colleges*), the interest soars, especially among alumni groups.

COMPETITION AND SPORTS PSYCHOLOGY

The interest of alumni in academic rankings mimics a parallel and often-rabid interest in intercollegiate sports rankings. Such intrigue is only excelled by devotion that many U.S. citizens have to the performances of professional sports teams. Thus, allusions to sorts and sports psychology are usually well received among general audiences. If you have developed particular insights through vocational or extended avocational interests, all the better.

Thus far, we have considered as presentation tools and materials—words and images. I would now like to turn our attention to physical objects—including sartorial accessories—that can be used to heighten drama and intrigue in talks.

Chapter Nine

Sartorial Accessories, Artifacts, and Props

What you wear and what you bring to presentations can become remarkable tools for enhancing drama and intrigue in talks. Because of the differing effects of these potential tools, let's consider them separately.

SARTORIAL ACCESSORIES

In his book on speech writing and public speaking, Jeff Cook (1989) notes "Be especially careful with props that must be worn. Anything you put on your body has the effect of saying, 'This is who I really am.'" This admonition is clearly true of certain people such as Patch Adams (the inspiration for the 1998 Robin Williams' film of the same name), who I once heard speak at a University of Connecticut commencement. Patch's legendary clown-like garb is truly a part of his personality and one would want to be circumspect about the messages sent by the uses of such unusual dress. However, I have found that sartorial accessories such as neckties—associated with the double entendre of "ties that bind"—can be used quite effectively to make points in presentations.

If you're a man, you probably love or hate neckties. I happen to love them and might even be a called a necktie collector. And, I love to wear them on occasions when I have to give a speech or otherwise address an audience. In these cases, the tie is chosen with a theme that accentuates the talk and the epilogue comment begins with, "Those who know me well, also know that I like to wear a necktie that embodies a theme integral to my overall presentation. Today I am wearing . . ."

Following are some examples of my sartorial references (see also figure 9.1):

- Presentations to faculty groups on research and scholarship in the arts and sciences have included references to a necktie containing detail from a Tiffany dragonfly design. The combination of artistic and technical talents of Louis Comfort Tiffany help me make a point about these different sides of creativity—often necessary for outstanding scholarship in both the arts and sciences.
- Talks on interdisciplinary research have been embellished by a necktie with illustrations of seventeenth and eighteen century French furniture design elements, which used *Ormolu* (from the French—*dorure d'or moulu*: "gilding with gold paste") or alloys that gained strength and beauty from the blending of elements, which is characteristic of notable interdisciplinary studies.
- My University of Arkansas necktie collection includes one with symbols of the Old Main tower, another with the University seal, and a third with a simulated autograph of J. William Fulbright. I have used these neckties to punctuate many presentations to prospective students and their parents, to faculty and student assemblages, to retired faculty and staff, and to alumni groups. The tower tie is used to make the point that the towers of the Old Main building (the University's first enduring structure, which was beautifully renovated in 1991) have been beacons of hope and pride for all Arkansans—beacons that have signaled—north and south—east and west—the academic strengths of the University.

  The University seal necktie affords the opportunity to talk about the University motto, *Veritate Duce Progredi*, which has been interpreted "to advance with truth as leader"—a particularly good message for prospective students.

  The Fulbright tie permits a recounting of the story of its namesake and his chance meeting on one of the sidewalks of the campus in 1924 with the University's graduate dean, John Clark Jordan. It was at that time when Jordan introduced the future President of the University of Arkansas (1939-1941), U. S. Congressman (1942-44), and five-term U.S. Senator (1944-1974) to the prospects of earning a Rhodes Scholarship (Woods 1995). This incident and my personal testimony of the uniqueness of the University's Senior Walk (with engravings of the names of more than 120,000 graduates [in 2003]) helps me make the point about the University's people-first philosophy, which has helped our faculty guide—so well—the intellectual and social development of generations of students.
- At memorial services I have worn a necktie depicting the great *fin de siecle* Scottish architect and artist Charles Rennie Mackintosh's "Rose and the Teardrop" design, which represents the joys and pathos of life and the mixed feelings that inevitably permeate memorial events.

Fig. 9.1. Examples of neckties used in talks to make dramatic or intriguing points: (1) Tiffany dragonfly design, (2) J. William Fulbright signature, (3) University of Arkansas seal, (4) University of Arkansas Old Main tower, (5) ormolu design, (6) Mackintosh rose and teardrop design; photo by Russell A. Cothren and layout design by Marsha June Smith (University of Arkansas logos depicted with permission)

My tie collection runs into the hundreds, and it would be boring for me to cover all the allusions I have developed with this neck-ware. Nevertheless, some additional necktie types and interesting allusions prompted by them are described in Appendix 9.

Before moving on from the discussion of the use of neckties in talks, let me add one further note. If you are using PowerPoint™ to guide or embellish a talk with a necktie allusion you can further augment the presentation through use of the optional screen, "My Father's Tie." You can then additionally enhance the effect by changing the colors of the necktie simulation on the left-hand side of the screen and colors in the text materials by customization (via the PowerPoint™ software and the options under the "Format" menu) and matching these slide features with the colors in your necktie. This little trick adds intrigue to your necktie-enhanced presentations.

Perhaps you are now tempted to ask: "How and where do you get such intriguing ties?" The selection of neckties should be integrated with your favorite themes or literary references. The best sources of unique neckties are museum shops, although I have found good candidates in retail stores near and far and sometimes in unlikely places, such as hotel shops.

If you are a woman, you may feel left out of the necktie game. Don't despair. Female colleagues at Spelman College and the University of Texas Medical Branch at Galveston have adopted parallel practices—using scarves (see also figure 9.2). A third female colleague at the University of Connecticut employs unique colors and patterns in suit jackets to illustrate epilogue points. A staff professional at the University of Arkansas has noted how she uses designs in dresses as reference points for comments during presentations.

So, whether you adopt the necktie game—or something analogous—consider "ties that bind" for connecting with audiences in special ways.

The uses of sartorial adjuncts to presentations need not be limited by the examples noted thus far.

If you have given a fair number of talks, you have certainly experienced the situation in which you are asked to address a group that has crafted a T-shirt with the group's logo or representation of a particular professional event. If you are given one of these T-shirts as part of your introduction, by all means consider putting it on as a prelude to your presentation. Few gestures will help you bond better with an audience than this dramatic act.

There are additional sartorial accessories that can be used to enhance drama and intrigue in talks. Consider, for example, lapel and other decorative pins and awareness ribbons.

Even before the horrific events of September 11, 2001 (the day that gave new meaning to the term "nine-one-one") in the United States, I wore lapel pins. Not just those of a patriotic variety—which have proliferated after

Fig. 9.2. Examples of scarves that could be used in talks to make dramatic or intriguing points: (1) Alice stories art, (2) Celtic design, (3) twelve-days of Christmas imagery, (4) Mackintosh rose and teardrop design; photo by Russell A. Cothren and layout design by Marsha June Smith (Photographic illustration of Alice Stories' scarf reproduced with permission of the Museum of Fine Arts, Boston)

9-11—but also institutional pins, pins commemorating certain artistic or architecturally significant works, and interesting logos.

Lapel pins come in a variety of types and quality. Following are the three major types, in descending quality order:

Cloisonné—developed from an art dating back to Mycenae in thirteenth century B.C.E. Greece, cloisonné (from the French for partition or compartment) work requires a carved-out base typically or one crafted from wires to provide the hollows that are filled with differently colored siliceous slurries. The nascent pin is fired to produce the enameled surface, which is finally polished and takes on an elegant look.

Photo Etched—produced by acid etching of pin stock, enameling and firing, photo etched pins are know for their clarity and detail.

Die Struck—using dies and soft metal—typically copper or iron—pins that are mass-produced through a stamping process akin to processes used for many centuries to produce coinage.

A great variety and number of lapel pins can be purchased from college book stores, museum shops, and Internet sources (e.g., PinTreasures.com; http://www.pintreasures.com/).

I wear "lapel pins," not only on jacket lapels, but also on turtleneck shirt collars (usually a bit left of center), shirt pockets, and badges that are issued at professional meetings or events. Why? Primarily because they provide clues to messages that I wish to portray formally and informally, but especially during talks.

Most universities, non-profit corporations, and for-profit companies have seals, symbols, and logos that are often crafted into lapel pins. The resulting pins offer symbolism that can be transformed into effective points in talks. Following are descriptions of a few of my favorites (see also figure 9.3):

- The official seals of the Universities of Connecticut and Arkansas (and no doubt many other universities) contain oak garlands or other representations of oak trees. It is intriguing to point out to audiences that the oak, from the time of ancient Greece, has been a symbol of wisdom, strength, and longevity. What better characteristics are there to associate with institutions of higher learning? What better characteristics to weave into talks about the growth and development of people and institutions?
- The University of Arkansas' Old Main towers are great symbols of academic excellence in Arkansas. And, you guessed it—the University has produced a tower pin, which I allude to often in presentations to students and prospective students and their parents.
- Flag pins became very popular in the United States following September 11th. I also like to collect friendship pins with flag depictions of two countries or a country and a state juxtaposed. Thus, I have pins with flag couplets such as: the U.S.A. and the State of Arkansas, the U.S.A. and Italy, and the U.S.A and South Africa, which commemorate or remind me of university partnerships, that I may wish to describe as a component of a presentation.
- On a recent trip to Italy, my wife found a pin depicting the design crafted by Michelangelo for the Piazza Campidoglio, which contains the Renaissance buildings that now house the Office of the Mayor of Rome and the Capitoline Art Museum. Michelangelo's web-like design reminds me of the scholarly inter-linkages associated with E. O. Wilson's (1998) concept of consilience and I have referred to it as a "web of understanding" when worn during talks in Italy and the United States.
- Living in Northwest Arkansas, I love to wear the Fayetteville High School pin, not only to show loyalty to our local partners in education but also because it embodies a beautiful representation of a Greek ionic column on a gorgeous violet background. The Greek representation of art and learning is a great prompt for talks to academic and general audiences about excellence in liberal arts education.

Since many audiences will include professionals who are affiliated with a variety of governmental, business, or professional organizations, or have unique

Fig. 9.3. Examples of lapel pins used in talks to make dramatic or intriguing points: (1) University of Arkansas pins: (a) football helmet with Razorback, (b) College of Engineering "Engine Hog", (c) running Razorback, (d) "class ring pin", (e) Old Main Tower pin, (2) Piazza Campidoglio pin from Rome, Italy, (3) Fayetteville, Ark. High School pin, (4) University of Connecticut pin; (5) Greek flag pin, (6) friendship flag pin: U.S.A./Greece, (7) Washington State University pin, (8) friendship flag pin: U.S.A./New York State, (9) awareness ribbon facsimile pin (pink—breast cancer); photo by Russell A. Cothren and original layout design by Marsha June Smith (Fayetteville High School. University of Arkansas, University of Connecticut, and Washington State University logos depicted with permission)

professional or social interests, you can undoubtedly think of seals, symbols, and logos that might have interesting characteristics for allusions in presentations. Some possible examples are referenced in Appendix 9, along with descriptions of lapel pins modeled after Awareness Ribbons (i.e., twists of ribbon worn on jacket lapels and exemplified by the pink twist crafted to prompt awareness of breast cancer victims and research). In the process of acquiring associated lapel pins and doing some background research, you might also develop a greater fondness for the roots of your own affiliations and interests.

Beyond lapel pins, you can imagine a host of other sartorial accessories from awareness ribbons per se to belts to caps to jackets to sweat shirts that embody interesting symbolism for references in talks. Just let your imagination run wild. Before leaving this chapter, however, let's explore the equally effective use of artifacts and props.

ARTIFACTS AND PROPS

Earlier, I noted how *objets d'art* could be used as special components of presentations. Artifacts and props, though somewhat more mundane, can also be used to heighten drama and intrigue. Let's consider them together.

You have likely been to meetings—especially lunches and dinners associated with professional gatherings—where the host organization provides a small gift—be it a lapel pin or something of greater worth. Have you noticed how many people can't keep their hands off of the gift during the subsequent event? The gift becomes a type of talisman—a connection object. Now imagine that you plan such a scenario, only using an object of your choosing—an object that ties into a message that you wish to imbue in the minds of audience members (see figure 9.4). This can work like magic.

Mary Ann Greenwood, president of a U. S. investment firm and a 9-11 World Trade Center survivor, has developed a novel way of using door keys in university and other non-profit agency fund-raising talks. She buys blank keys, sometimes with a logo or colorful plastic insert, and a single key is positioned at the place of every person attending her talk. During the talk, she asks members of her audience to pick up their key and think of it as a symbol of their commitment to the fund-raising goals of the organization she is representing. She then asks the audience members—who may already be committed to a fund-raising project—to place the key on their key chain as a reminder of the larger fund-raising effort and its goals.

One can imagine adopting Greenwood's tactic in a variety of settings to make parallel points. You might also imagine employing other small objects that can be used in intriguing symbolic ways. For example, the Sam M. Walton

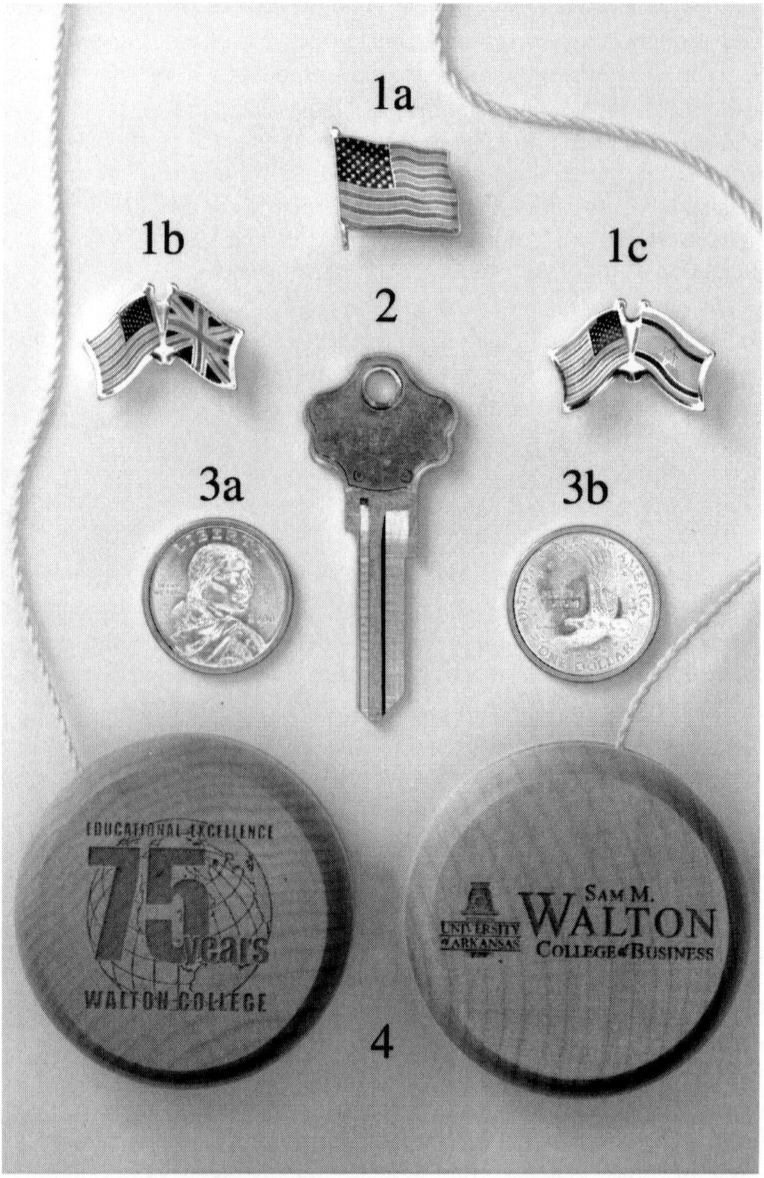

Fig. 9.4. Examples of "prop gifts" used in talks to make dramatic or intriguing points: (1) Lapel Pins: (a) American flag pin, (b) U.S.A./Great Britain friendship flag pin, (c) U.S.A./Israel friendship flag pin, (2) key blank, (3 a and b) Sacagawea dollars, (4) Walton College Yo-Yo's; photo by Russell A. Cothren and original layout design by Marsha June Smith(Walton College and University of Arkansas logos depicted with permission)

College of Business at the University of Arkansas recently had an alumni, donor, and student commemorative event to mark the 75th anniversary of the College. Doyle Williams, the Dean of the College, had wooden Yo-Yo's crafted and positioned at each attendee's place. The Yo-Yo's bore the seal of the college on one side and the 75-year symbolism on the other (see figure 9.4). During the Dean's introductory remarks, he noted that the Yo-Yo (while invented in China more than 1,000 years ago) was manufactured in its now popular form and marketed in the United States at about the time of the founding of the Walton College. He then went on to note the endearing qualities of this toy—its ready fit into one's pocket and its ability to return to its owner. He then shared his hope that such endearment and "will to return" would always parallel sentiments among his college's alumni.

In 2002, I attended a luncheon presentation given by General Wesley Clark and organized by the Springdale, Arkansas Chamber of Commerce. Because of the nature of General Clark's remarks (homeland security), he requested that the Chamber purchase American flag lapel pins for all guests. Thus, at each place was a handsome cloisonné pin, accentuated by red, white, and blue table decorations and bunting about the room. The setting and decorations, accentuated by the lapel pins, added great value to General Clark's fine presentation.

There are undoubtedly many other objects that would support meaningful allusions, metaphors, and talking points. For example, how about miniature flags or friendship flag pins—representing an emerging partnership with another state, country, or organization? What about awareness ribbons, lapel pins, or pencils or business card holders? The list is seemingly endless.

Organizations that invite you to speak may be willing to purchase items as enumerated. Many of these objects—particularly when purchased in bulk—are fairly inexpensive. For options and sources of awareness ribbons and lapel pins see Appendix 9.

Other artifacts—used effectively in talks—include congratulatory or critical letters or copies of recent magazines or newspapers containing references or articles relevant to your presentation. I have also used short audio recordings to make points, including one time when I asked a student member of the prospective audience to record—for playing—a sentence in French that I wished to have spoken by someone fluent in the language.

Buzz Aldrin, one of the first Astronauts to walk on the moon (along with Neil Armstrong in July of 1969), begins talks with the public display of a Buzz Lightyear Doll (from the character of the same name in the Disney film, *Toy Story*).

John White, National Science Board member and Chancellor of the University of Arkansas, uses imaginary nanoparticles sprinkled on the face of a lit overhead projector to make the point about their sub-microscopic size. For a contrasting allusion, who can forget President Reagan's address to Congress where he stood by a "mountain" of U.S. budget books and referred to the assemblage as a "behemoth".

Nancy Talburt, detective novel scholar, has suggested the use of Matryoshka (Russian nesting) dolls (see figure 9.5) as a metaphor for the unveiling of truth in stories of intrigue and presentations thereof. This is a fascinating idea that she concocted from the opening sequence used in the television production of John le Carre's (1974) *Tinker, Tailor, Soldier, Spy*, some years ago.

In Chapter 1, I alluded to a joint effort of the University of Washington (UW) and Washington State University (WSU) to convince the Washington Legislature of the wisdom of investing in an Advanced Technology Initiative (ATI). As a part of this initiative, Bob Miller of the UW and I made a series of presentations to the Washington State House and Senate Commerce and Labor, Higher Education, and Trade and Economic Development Committees on the features and proposed merits of this multi-million dollar proposal. Briefly, we were attempting to make the case that modern university-based researchers are capable of not only doing good basic research, but also assisting the start-up of high technology companies, which could be of great economic benefit to the Evergreen State. For use during the joint presentations, we chose artifacts that exemplified the types of value-added products that result from research.

The UW-derived artifact was a vial containing what appeared to be a sample of water. But, as Bob Miller held the vial in his hand extended above his head, he noted to the state representatives and senators that the apparent water-white liquid was actually a solution of a reagent discovered and developed by a researcher in the UW Medical School—a reagent highly valuable in the diagnosis of osteoporosis.

The WSU-derived artifact was a sample of what appeared to be an "angel-hair" like product that one might find on a Christmas tree. However, the product was actually a siliceous material that was derived from basalt rock (abundant in Eastern Washington) by a unique process discovered and developed by a WSU engineering professor. You can imagine the legislators' fascinated looks when samples of basalt rock and the angel-hair product were held up side by side. The fascination increased when I described the economic potential of the product as a fire-resistant and environmentally safe insulation of possible interest to the U.S. Navy.

The impact of the UW and WSU artifacts was further enhanced when we circulated them among the legislators for their closer inspection. I can recall one legislator remarking, "How do people come up with things like this?" That is a reflection of true drama and intrigue.

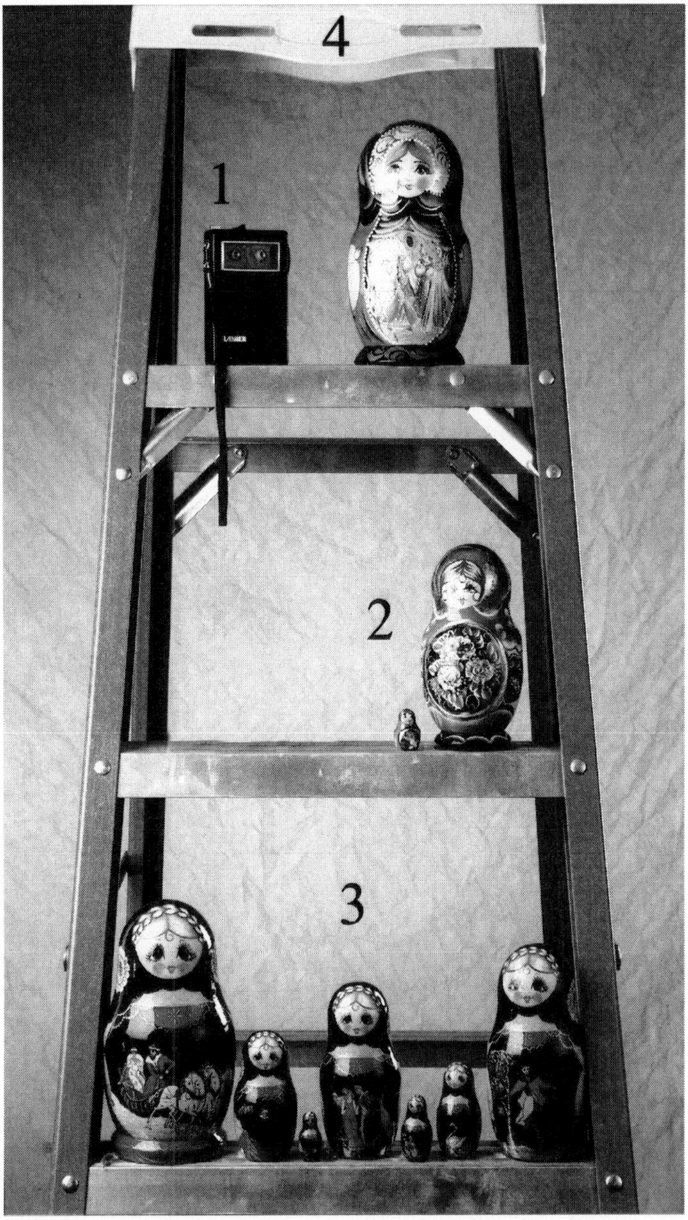

Fig. 9.5. Examples of props used in talks to make dramatic or intriguing points: (1) hand-held tape recorder, (2 and 3) Matryoshka Dolls, (4) step-ladder; photo by Russell A. Cothren and original layout design by Marsha June Smith

In Appendix 7, I recommend the great Antoine de Saint-Exupéry's book, *The Little Prince* (1943), as a source of dramatic and intriguing allusions to the characteristics of profound friendship. When I quote from or otherwise reference Saint-Exupéry's book in talks, I take out of my pockets—for display—Little Prince statuettes that I purchased in Lyon, France (see: http://www.karikter.com/html/prince.html). Other props and artifacts referred to above are depicted in figure 9.5.

Besides artifacts, consider other props to add drama and intrigue to presentations.

When Nelson Rockefeller was Governor of New York, he reportedly had a sizable desk in his office with an apparent set of drawers that pulled out to make a stepladder. When the Press Corps came to see him, he would dramatically reach down, pull out the seeming set of drawers, ceremoniously climb the stepladder onto the top of his desk from where he could address his visitors and subsequently answer questions.

I have used permutations on the "Rockefeller technique" by standing on desktops or chairs, prior to addressing groups. Of course, I always remove my shoes first lest I mar a desk surface or soil a chair cushion. The act of removing your shoes in and of itself is perceived dramatically.

Another permutation on this theme is to climb a six-to-eight foot stepladder before making a short set of remarks. After so doing, you can refer—for interest—to the use of a stepladder as one of only a few props that was used in the original Broadway production of Thornton Wilder's Pulitzer Prize winning production of *Our Town* in 1938 (Brantley 2001).

During one time when I used the "stepladder technique," I had a colleague come up to me afterwards to say, "I thought you had lost your mind when you brought out that stepladder." Another more admiring colleague confessed the thought, "Where's my ladder?" Now, that's truly dramatic.

Besides standing on chairs, I have picked up on a trick that many prominent media professionals use when handling questions after a talk. Take a nearby chair that may have a low back and consider turning it around to allow you to crouch a bit and rest your derriere on the top of the chair back. The effect is one of relaxation but it also places you just slightly above seated members of the audience. Additionally, it saves your feet.

You can probably imagine other props that might prove to be wonderful additions to presentations. After having read and seen the film based on the first Harry Potter book, I imagine we'll soon see speakers using wands for effect.

We've now assembled a cache of tools and materials that are readily available to build drama and intrigue into your presentations. You should now feel empowered to take the next step—the crafting of talks. The excitement will build as we bring the tools and materials together in ways that you and I know will engage and enthrall our audiences.

Section Three

CRAFTING PRESENTATIONS

Akin to a capital construction project, preparing presentations requires planning, the selection of tools and materials, and the actual crafting of the final masterpiece. It is now time to think about the melding of the elements in Sections I and II with finishing materials and processes to craft the "structures" of presentations—a varying combination of scripts, notes, audio or videotapes, PowerPoint™ presentations, sartorial accessories, and props. We'll save Section IV for ideas and techniques that should prove useful in the delivery of oral presentations.

In this third section of our overall effort, we'll consider guidelines for preparing presentations that engage audiences in dramatic and intriguing ways. The guidelines are organized under the headings: (1) presentation approaches, (2) defining purposes and choosing topics, titles, and themes, (3) crafting presentation content, (4) insuring finishing touches. These headings serve as the bases for the four chapters of Section III.

Chapter Ten

Presentation Approaches

Active professionals are witness to varying approaches to presentations. The most common approaches are categorized as follows:

- Preparing full-text talks for verbatim presentation—with or without a teleprompter
- Preparing outlines—perhaps with some complete sentences—that are used as reference during oral presentations
- Winging it—working from key words or themes that guide remarks
- Any one of the above, only guided and assisted by sets of slides, overhead transparencies, or PowerPoint™ presentations—along with artwork, sartorial accessories, artifacts or props

Thus, there are several common approaches to presentations and perhaps you have used them all—as I have—at one time or another. Also, you probably recognize the advantages and drawbacks to each. Thus, in choosing an approach, you have to consider personal perspectives and the comfort level afforded to you and your audience through the different approaches. Contemplating approaches for particular settings, you might consider the following ideas.

First, unless there is a reason for a tight scripting of remarks (e.g., participating in segments of official ceremonies such as commencements or convocations where precise timing is of great importance or in cases of presentations of policies of government agencies or other institutions), avoid verbatim readings. However, in those instances where you must use verbatim remarks, consider the following advice:

- Prepare the remarks on 8½ × 11 in. white notebook paper with 18- to 24-font type.

- Do not type text over more than two-thirds of the top portion of each sheet of paper so that your head does not have to nod down too deeply while reading the presentation.
- Insert the ordered sheets into plastic sleeves that can be positioned into a ring binder. After the top sheet, consider inserting subsequent sheets into sleeves in a contiguous manner so that—in mid-talk—two sheets face one another—one on the left and one on the right-hand side of the opened ring binder. This trick helps to minimize the turning of pages during the talk and allows, while you are reading from the left hand sheet, glancing ahead to the next section of the talk.
- If you use a teleprompter, make sure the person operating the system understands the pace of the talk and is sensitized to pauses that you may take during the presentation.
- If the verbatim presentation is integrated with slides, overhead transparencies, or plates from a PowerPoint™ presentation, be sure to put "slide prompts" in the text—preferably in a different color or font to differentiate them from the text being read.

I avoid verbatim presentations. They crimp spontaneity, tend to signal that someone else wrote your talk, and force you to speak from a podium, which creates a barrier between you and your audience. You will also find that audiences containing younger people—in particular—are less attentive to verbatim presentations.

So, assuming we avoid verbatim presentations, what other tips are useful in adopting alternative approaches to presentations? Let's consider further the outline and winging-it approaches mentioned earlier.

If you have to give a short set of remarks (i.e., three-to-five minutes), consider working from a three (preferably) or four words or points prepared in 18- to 24-typefont on 8½ × 11 in. paper or 3 × 5 in. index cards. Detz (1992) notes an almost archetypical significance to the number three and its use in concepts and beliefs. Manifestations include threesome-sets of words such as the three primary virtues (faith, hope, and charity), the Christian trinity (Father, Son, and Holy Spirit), components of the earth day (morning, mid-day, and night), the three branches of U.S. and many state governments (executive, legislative, and judiciary), and elements of U.S. state (e.g., Georgia: wisdom, justice, and moderation) and national Constitutions (life, liberty, and the pursuit of happiness). I have referred in talks to the latter as elements of America's democratizing morality and compared them to the great triptychs of other governing documents such as the French Constitution (i.e., liberty, equality, and fraternity).

The "rule of three" has been used by countless numbers of speakers in speeches—famous and not so famous. For example, who can forget Douglas McArthur's 1962 farewell speech to West Point—the so-called "Long Grey Line" speech, which resounds in many a memory with the words "Duty, Honor, Country."

If you expand your approach from singular words to three or four points, they need only involve a few words lest you be tempted to read from your notes. It can not be overemphasized that while you will want audiences to perceive that you are well prepared, they also appreciate the sense of spontaneity and genuineness that comes through when remarks are not read.

Best of all, if you can "wing-it"—provide remarks without notes—you'll perceive great appreciation among audience members. The biggest challenge in "winging-it" is staying disciplined—not rambling or trying to say too much. Thus, speakers who "wing-it" will often settle on three words that guide their remarks and try to be conscious of timing. A confederate in the audience can also be asked to time your remarks and to give you a "sign" when the pre-agreed time is up.

Another option, particularly for longer talks (i.e., five-to-fifty minutes), involves working from no notes other than those incorporated into slides, overhead transparencies, or PowerPoint™ presentations. There are a number of advantages to this approach, including:

- Enhancing chances for spontaneity
- Affording opportunities to come out from behind the podium and address audiences with your voice amplified through a hand-held or lapel microphone (see also Section IV)
- Effectively illustrating presentations through visually impressive images, sounds, and animation

All of the above advantages assist in building drama and intrigue into presentations. And, if you are speaking to audiences composed of adolescents or thirty-somethings, you'll find much greater appreciation for such an approach *versus* the reading of text.

So, it is clearly your preference but consider choosing a presentation approach that will enhance your opportunities to engage audiences in dramatic and intriguing ways. With the presentation approach chosen, it is now time to define purposes and select topics, titles, and themes for presentations.

Chapter Eleven

Defining Purposes and Choosing Titles, Topics, and Themes of Presentations

The purpose of a talk will help to define a topic and some possible themes. As noted in Section I, it is important to determine the expectations, interests, and current projects of audiences and groups they represent.

Jeary (1997) suggests four purposes of presentations: (1) imparting information, (2) teaching, (3) persuasion, (4) entertainment or some combination of the above. I would also add a fifth, "inspiration" and suggest that most talks serve all five purposes. Indeed, for most occasions, wouldn't we want audience members—having heard your presentation—saying things such as: "I really learned something from that talk.", "The speaker truly displayed an ability to get points across.", "There were some persuasive points made by the speaker.", "I greatly enjoyed that presentation," and "That presentation was inspiring." So, how might these thoughts guide our choice of a topic and themes?

The topic should dovetail with the prospective audience's interests, but may be dictated by a suggestion you receive as a part of an invitation to speak or an obvious connection you have with your place of employment or other organization. For example, having served in several central administrative posts at universities, I have given many talks on the future of these institutions. As noted previously, "future-oriented topics" are fascinating to audiences. Equally engaging are topics that embrace analyses of events of specific interest to audiences. For example, environmental catastrophes, epidemics, and incidences involving labor relations will interest audiences consisting of social activists. Topics pertaining to the historic, social, and cultural context of movements or civilizations related to an audience's interest are also great topics.

The best advice is to find out all you can about the audience's interests, background, and current efforts; then craft a dramatic and intriguing topic. If you need additional help, consider using the Allyn & Bacon Public Speaking

Website (http://www.abacon.com/pubspeak/), which contains URLs for a host of topic-oriented websites under the headings: General Topics, Science, Health and Technology, Societal Problems, Legislative Matters, and Legal and Judicial Questions.

With a topic chosen, think about a title and some themes or sub-topics that might fit under that topic. The title is important because it is the "hook" that lures audience attendance and participation.

Fletcher Dean, the author and developer of the speech writing newsletter, *OnSpeechwriting*, recently published a column (Dean 2003) on the significance of titles and principles that are helpful in crafting effective titles. Dean's "principles" include the use of alliteration, altered clichés, a question, attention-grabbing words, numbers, rhymes, triplets, unique wording, or some combination of the aforementioned. I would add the use of double entendre and references to literature and popular culture. Following are titles of talks (and, in parentheses, examples of audiences) I have given that incorporate one or more of Dean's "principles."

Alliteration: "Pedestals, Parapets and Pits—A Model for Academic Scholarly Life" (Association of Faculty Women, Washington State University, Pullman, Wash., 1996)

Altered Clichés: "International Students Make a World of Difference at the University of Arkansas" (University of Arkansas International Student Orientation, Fayetteville, Ark., 2000)

A Question: "Critical Technologies—How Critical Are They?" (Critical Technologies Conference, Hartford, Conn., 1998)

Attention-Grabbing Words: "Extinguishing Burnout—Hope for the Mid-Level Professional" (Upjohn Company, Kalamazoo, Mich., 1984)

Double Entendre: "The Promise of a New Position" (University of Arkansas Staff Senate, Fayetteville, Ark., 2000)

Numbers: "The Twelve Days of Christmas in Story and Song" (Faculty Winter Holiday Party, University of Arkansas, Fayetteville, Ark., 2002)

References to Literature and Popular Culture: "Where Have You Gone Joe DiMaggio? Ethics and Graduate Research" (Pharmacology/Toxicology Graduate Program, Washington State University, Pullman, Wash., 1991)

"Through the Looking-Glass: Graduate Education and Its Future" (Far Eastern State University, Vladivostok, Russia, 1992)

"Graduate Research—A Guide for the Perplexed" (School of Fisheries, University of Washington, Seattle, Wash., 1996)

"Following the Yellow Brick Road—The University of Connecticut's Contributions to the Economy of Connecticut and Beyond" (Integrating Economics—A Fellowship Seminar for Teachers, University of Connecticut, Storrs, Conn., 1998)

"Time in a Bottle" (Farewell Address, University of Connecticut, Storrs, Conn., 2000)

Rhymes: "Studying Locally—Thinking Globally" (Office of International Affairs, American English Language Instruction Program Alumni Dinner, University of Connecticut, Storrs, Conn., 2000)

Triplets: "Games, Games, Games . . . of Life." (University of Arkansas, College of Education and Health Professions Graduation Recognition Ceremony, Fayetteville, Ark., 2002)

Unique Wording: "From Apricots to Microchips: Technology Transfer at Washington State University" (University of Washington Technology Transfer Committee, Seattle, Wash., 1992)

With a title chosen, you will need to think about themes or sub-topics. For example, a "future oriented" topic begs for sub-topics such as: Where are we now? How did we get to where we are? Where might we go from here?

As another example, topics on advances in science and technology would suggest themes such as: What led to the advance? How might it be of importance to society today? What may this advance mean to future discoveries? The splitting of topics into sub-topics provides a convenient segue to Chapter 12 and the actual crafting of presentation content.

Chapter Twelve

Crafting Presentation Content

Having original ideas for topics, titles, and sub-topics or themes provides an extremely powerful start to crafting a talk. For example, in my life as a chemist, I might have been asked by the president of a high school chemistry club to give a talk on solvent extraction, including the use of ethyl ether as an extraction solvent. I might think of starting with some anecdotes, such as the original use of ethyl ether as an anesthetic, which would help make a point about the solvent's volatility. Or, I might allude to the well-known twentieth century entertainer who scarred himself for life because he did not respect the extreme flammability of ethyl ether.

I would also follow the advice in Chapter 7—liberally defining terms and drawing analogies to commonly observed phenomenon. Terms important to this talk would include the specific gravity or mass of ethyl ether and other extraction solvents relative to water, which, for many solvents, is less than water thereby causing a typical extraction solvent to appear at the top of a container holding similar portions of solvent and water. The term "immiscibility" would also be important—namely, the fact that ethyl ether and many other extraction solvents are not mixable in all proportions with water.

Continuing with the advice from Chapter 7, I could draw an analogy between ethyl ether or similar solvent and water mixtures and oil and vinegar mixtures that we use commonly as salad dressings. The audience will then begin to conjure up mental pictures of vessels containing separated layers of liquids. They may also begin to perceive the possible power of solvents such as ethyl ether to draw substances—such as high solvent affinity pharmaceuticals—from one layer to the other (typically from the water to the ether layer) based on relative affinities of these compounds in one medium *versus* the other. To end the talk, I might add a description of the modern use of liquid gases (e.g., carbon dioxide) as extraction aids and point out how many of these newer extraction media are much less toxic to humans, much more friendly to the environment, and non-flammable. These are some of the things that would come to my mind in the early organization of what could become an intriguing talk—at least for chemistry students.

But, coming this far—by example—I would want next to improve the organization of my approach. Thus, I would step back and consider systematic organization of the material just "penned-out" from my "stream of consciousness" thoughts. The systematic approach can be broken into three steps: (1) getting ideas, (2) expansion and development of topics and sub-topics, (3) refining the content of the presentation. Each of these steps will be delineated in the following pages.

GETTING IDEAS

The crafting of presentation content is not unlike the writing of articles. As you prepare for presentations you'll often find that inspiration comes at unusual times. The section you just read about the hypothetical ethyl ether talk was inspired by thoughts that occurred very early on a February morning. The presentation had been on my mind the previous day and it is likely that it was also in my thoughts when I fell asleep that night. Upon waking, some very good ideas came to mind as though even in my sleep my mind was crafting the presentation for which I was preparing. This kind of inspiration is typical for many people.

Stories abound about insight resulting from the interplay of the conscious and sub-conscious minds. Psychologist Julian Jaynes (1976) referred to the 3 Bs—the bed, the bath, and the bus—to describe times of fresh insight occurring immediately before or after periods of rest and personal hygiene, or when traveling.

Examples of the influence of the 3 Bs include the timing of Walt Rostow's inspiration for a 1983 book on economics: "At 3:00 on the morning of December 15, 1982, when sleep was light, I got up and outlined this book in just about the form that it now appears." A train trip stimulated Karl Folkers' imagining a correct structural formula for penicillin: "On the train from Chicago to Madison, I sat there, looking out the window . . . As I reviewed the evidence in my mind about the *beta*-lactam formulas, they sounded pretty good . . . . It was on that trip that for the first time in my participation in the penicillin program, that I really took the *beta*-lactam seriously" (Sheehan 1982). Jean François Champollion's first insight into the deciphering of the Rosetta Stone occurred during a coach trip to Paris in 1807 (Ceram 1982).

The effects of the 3 Bs apply to thoughtful people, regardless of their background in the arts, humanities, or sciences. An anthropologist friend of mine believes like Melville that, "meditation and water are wedded for ever" because of the great ideas he has had while bathing (Smith 1998). Henry David Thoreau (1854) undoubtedly understood intuitively the influence of the 3 Bs when he wrote, "Morning brings back the heroic ages . . . Then there is least somnolence in us; and for an hour, at least, some part of us awakes which slumbers all the rest of the day and night."

Other creative people have been influenced analogously by the 3 Bs and have been known to conjure up some of their best ideas while traveling to and from professional meetings. Oddly enough, as the astronauts had to leave the earth to see its grandeur for the "first time," ideas for presentations frequently arise by metaphorically "leaving" them alone—or at least allowing some passage of time for ideas to emerge and re-emerge.

Having had some good ideas, reducing them to writing, and allowing time for the ideas to linger in your mind, it is important next to work purposefully on the topic and sub-topics.

EXPANSION AND DEVELOPMENT OF TOPICS AND THEMES

Let's presume that you've settled on a topic and some ideas for sub-topics. How might we systematically develop presentation content?

There are several ways to use your topics and sub-topics to craft interesting, dramatic, and intriguing presentation content. Some methods are tried and true—others are less conventional. Here, in outline fashion, are my favorites:

- Historically Linking Themes: start with important events of the day or year and link them to the topic and sub-topics; or, use the approach: (1) here's where we are (2) here's how we got here, (3) here's where we are going; or, link timelines and historically important days and events to guide topic development
- Archetypal Stories: use an archetypal tale (e.g., hero's journey), event or imagery (e.g., the archetypes of the hearth and the ocean or other bodies of water) to craft story-based presentations
- Analytical Approach: akin to a media reporter's modus operandi, ask the proverbial, "what," "when," "where," "how," and "why" questions about a topic
- Imagining Approach: start with three imagining questions that help you "walk the audience through" the sub-topics

With all approaches, it is important to avoid being overly ambitious. In fact, for most talks, I would be hesitant to cover more than three sub-topics. The triple sub-topics can be sub-divided into major components but be careful of trying to cover too much. Remember the adage that "beginning teachers try to tell their students everything they know"; and, the admonishment of Voltaire, "The secret of being a bore is to tell everything." If you make such attempts you'll surely fail, since most audiences can only absorb and remember limited amounts of material. With that caveat in mind, let's explore the approaches enumerated above.

HISTORICALLY LINKING THEMES

Chapter 6 contains a description and examples (table 6.1) of linking subtopics and ideas with historic events of the day. I have also used major historic anniversaries as good reference points for themes; the bicentennial of the Lewis and Clark Expedition being one of these (see also Chapters 1 and 6). Other anniversary references—typically a decade, multiple decades, centuries, or millennia—provide great references that may be related to themes in dramatic and intriguing ways. For example, the sixty-year anniversary of the first major computer or ENIAC (for *electronic numerical integrator and computer*) in 2006, offers a good reference point for talks that might be based on the remarkable advances in computer science and technology during a six-decade period.

Alternative historically-linked approaches can be directed by the subtopics "here's where we are; here's how we got here; here's where we are going," which can be correlated to past decades, centuries, or eras. Jack McGuire (1998), in his book on storytelling, suggests the use of notable historic events to engage audiences in special ways. Asking audience members to close their eyes and think about where they were when President Kennedy was assassinated (1963), when President Richard Nixon resigned (1974), when the United States celebrated its bicentennial (1996), when Princess Diana was killed tragically in an automobile accident (1997), or when terrorist flown planes struck the World Trade Center in New York and the Pentagon in Washington, DC (2001), mentally positions people at a place and time in history that can serve as a dramatic launching pad for contextual information that is incorporated into presentations. For example, speaking about the environmental movement that began with the original Earth Day, April 22, 1970, could be introduced with a thoughtful statement such as, "just about nine months after Neil Armstrong and Buzz Aldrin stepped onto the moon . . . ".

The confluence of art and science at critical points in history also provides a wonderful framework for presentations. The great U.S. Smithsonian exhibit in 1992—entitled *Circa 1492* (Levinson 1991) provides a wonderful example. The exhibit, which included artifacts, dioramas, text, charts, and works of art, portrayed the interplay of art, science, and geopolitics across the world 500 years earlier, coinciding of course, with the first landing of Columbus on islands near what is now the Dominican Republic and Haiti. The exhibit's effectiveness in integrating a momentous period of exploration with arts and sciences offered dramatic and intriguing insights into late fifteenth and early sixteenth centuries' cross-cultural influences that undoubtedly fascinated many who attended this highly successful exhibit.

Looking for ways to link history and historically important periods to your speeches and presentations should not be overlooked as you craft your talk. These methods, along with the use of archetypal stories considered next, will keep your audience intrigued and your presentation lively.

ARCHETYPAL STORIES

Taken from the Greek *archetypos* or "original pattern," archetypes represent recurring story patterns, ideas, and symbolism that have been proposed as manifestations of what the great twentieth century psychologist Carl Jung called the collective unconscious. Regardless of whether audience members relate to Jungian thought or not, the use of archetypically crafted material offers subtle opportunities to make presentations come to life.

Some of the archetypes that work best involve references to heroic stories and archetypal elements such as the hearth, oceans, or other bodies of water. Archetypal stories that embody these elements and secrets or fantasies, especially from childhood or journeys—figurative or literal—are particularly effective. In the time-in-the-bottle talk noted earlier (Chapter 6), for example, the message of savoring ones' memories in special ways has great appeal to audiences. This appeal is heightened by the revelation of a childhood fantasy about tossing message-laden bottles into the sea. Audience intrigue can be further heightened when such a talk is first given and you can say honestly, "I have never shared this before with an audience." For some time later, you will also be able to admit honestly "I have shared this fantasy with few people (or audiences)."

Travel by you, by prominent people you have known, or those you have learned about through biographies can have very powerful archetypal effects on audiences. I have satisfyingly used portrayals of travel experiences many times in talks. A recent presentation to a Model Arab League offers a good example.

The King Fahd Center for Middle East and Islamic Studies at the University of Arkansas had—for several years—offered an educational and outreach event that engaged high school students and their teachers in a special activity. The students, through the guidance of their high school teachers, were asked in groups to study about particular Middle Eastern countries—their cultures, political systems, and views, and their current sociopolitical positions in the world. The country teams were then convened on the University campus in a Model Arab League, wherein the groups—informed through their studies—debated issues important to the Middle East.

My assignment in 2001 was to address the League, prior to its major session on a Saturday morning. I used the opportunity to give a talk entitled, "Being a Scholar—Being a Diplomat," to speak about scholarship, in general, and to contrast the work of politicians and diplomats. I also offered several thoughts on how scholarship and diplomacy are informed by travel—figuratively and literally.

The talk was given through a PowerPoint™ presentation that was illustrated with map and flag representations of countries represented at the Model Arab League session. The map and flag representations were obtained from the U. S. Central Intelligence Agency (CIA) website, *The World Fact Book* (http://www.odci.gov/cia/publications/factbook/index.html).

I ended the talk with a short survey of several countries I have worked in as a part of my career and how projects in those countries were pivotal in shaping my views about university student and program development. These slides, akin to their Middle Eastern counterparts, were illustrated with map and flag representations from the countries noted in my "personal journey."

The presentation was a hit. In part, because it had the archetypal elements of the "hero's journey"—venturing forward, facing challenges, and gaining insights, and returning to the home front to affect changes.

Be sure to consider archetypal elements that may serve as themes in presentations. And do think of personal admissions that may enhance drama and intrigue in talks. Such drama and intrigue is also heightened by the "what," "where," "when," "how," and "why" questions imbedded in the approach to be considered next.

ANALYTICAL APPROACH

Answering the proverbial "what," "when," "where," "how," and "why" questions of a topic, is probably one of the surest ways of crafting a talk. Think, for example, of a talk prepared to describe the findings of a report of a state, national, or institutional commission. You can readily imagine how the talk might proceed with answers and illustrations to the following questions:

- What is the nature of the commission?
- When and why was the commission formed?
- What—in some detail—was found by the commission?
- What are the recommendations of the commission?
- What happens—now—to the commission and its work?

I have given countless talks of this type and could cite several examples from this set of experiences. I thought, however, that I'd share with you a short description of a wonderful talk that is given by Stanford University's Paul Mortfield (Education and Outreach Coordinator of the Stanford University Solar On-Line Activity Resources [SOLAR] Center) to primary and secondary students and teachers. The SOLAR Center represents a major effort by Stanford faculty, students, and staff to study our solar system's star—the sun. The work includes acquisition and analysis of data derived from NASA's Solar and Heliospheric Observatory (SOHO), which was launched in December 1995 but in 2002, continued to send data to earth, well past its anticipated lifetime.

Mortfield's talk is supported by a PowerPoint™ presentation complete with still and time-lapse photographic imagery—accessible in real time to demonstrate the dynamics of spacecraft (e.g., SOHO itself) movements relative to planets and comets and activities of the sun's surface, including solar flares and coronas. Briefly, some of the "what," "when," "where," "how," and "why" features of the talk are as follows:

- What is SOLAR and SOHO? What are some of the known characteristics of the sun (e.g., age, size, temperature)?
- When was SOHO launched? And, when did the speaker become involved, including allusions to boyhood fantasies about space science? When will the SOHO mission be complete?
- Where is the SOLAR project headed from here?
- How will scientists use information gathered from SOHO?
- Why is it important to study the sun, including its effects on telecommunications, space exploration, weather, and the magnetic fields of the earth and other planets of our solar system?

Mortfield completes his SOLO talk with a description of challenges that were faced by scientists when the SOHO probe was nearly lost due to gyroscope failures in 2000. He also ends with an elaboration of the importance of the SOHO mission relative to future projects including astronaut-based missions to Mars. The combination of enthusiasm and excitement that Mortfield exudes for his life's interests and research adds the kind of drama and intrigue we all seek in developing and giving presentations. His particular approach to topic and sub-topic development represents aptly the Analytical Approach, which involves the interplay of terse questions and more elaborate answers and is commonly and effectively employed in crafting talks.

Another approach using questions involves an imagining process to frame a topic and sub-topics.

IMAGINING APPROACH

Akin to talks on "the future," audiences are fascinated with visioning or imagining new concepts, new projects, and new programs. The Imagining Approach builds on this enthusiasm by beginning a presentation with three imagining scenarios that become the themes for the talk.

I have used the Imagining Approach several times, but most effectively in describing partnerships, in my case, involving universities and institutions or corporations in the private sector. A specific example includes a partnership in animal vaccine research that the University of Connecticut was trying to develop with a major U.S. pharmaceutical company. Among the project's goals were the intention to build a state-of-the art facility and provide opportunities for University students and faculty to work side-by-side with industry researchers. The talk, crafted to build support for the project began with the following three "imagining scenarios":

- Imagine world-class research leading to new vaccines for the prevention of livestock-unique diseases that compromise food safety, farm animal welfare, and agricultural animal production costs.
- Imagine this pathbreaking research conducted collaboratively among university faculty, students, and scientists of one of the world's largest pharmaceutical companies.
- Imagine all of these activities in a state-of-the-art facility in the quiet corner (the northeast quadrant) of Connecticut.

As noted through this example, the scenarios start globally but proceed subsequently to more specific visions. Through the latter, you can engage the audience in a dramatic and intriguing manner, by including their participation—figuratively—in the visions portrayed.

Now that you have developed your topic and sub-topics, you'll need to use some of the tools and materials outlined in Section II as well as those that can be accessed through library and Internet sources to craft the combination of scripts, notes, audio or videotapes, PowerPoint™ presentations, sartorial accessories, and props that become the "structure" of your presentation. Before calling the project complete, however, you'll want to consider finishing touches—opening comments, outline, summary remarks, and what I will refer to as *lagniappes*. The finishing touches are considered in the next and final chapter of Section III.

Chapter Thirteen

Finishing Touches

Paraphrasing Aristotle, excellence in any endeavor is not a single effort but a series of outstanding efforts—so too with presentations. And, the finishing touches: physical appearance and opening comments (great beginnings), the outline and ending summary (the bookends of the talk), and the little delectable extra at the very end (the *lagniappe* [pronounced "lan-yapp"]) add measurably to an excellent whole. Let's consider each of this items in turn.

GREAT BEGINNINGS

The proverbial "power of first impression" is as true in speech making as it is in other human interactions. How you appear, how you walk to the podium or center stage, and the first words out of your mouth—all affect the initial engagement with the audience. It is possible to recover from a poor beginning but crafting a "great beginning" is easy.

Start with dress. Choose a smart outfit for the occasion. I use the word "smart" as a double entendre. The outfit need not cost a fortune but it ought to be neat and tasteful—suits and jackets and slacks for men, business suits or other professional garb for women. Suits work well when appearing before most business groups, but may not work so well among other assemblages. Indeed, there are certain occasions when overdressing can be a detriment. For example, I suggest that overdressing can actually hamper the effectiveness of testimony to a state legislative committee or panel. My best advice? Leave the pin striped suits and the fancy watches at home if you are speaking to a group whose economic means are modest. I even avoid suits when speaking before faculty and student groups.

In Chapter 9, we considered the use of sartorial accessories, including the wearing of lapel pins and awareness ribbons. One note is in order relative to this section on overall attire. When displaying lapel pins and awareness ribbons, or name badges, for that matter, on a suit jacket lapel, choose the left lapel, if you wish the greatest notice by people you address. If you are right handed, there is a tendency to place a lapel pin or name tag on one's right lapel. However, akin to newspaper advertisers' advise about the effectiveness of the northeast quadrant of a tabloid page, there is a tendency for persons to look at the upper right hand quadrant of objects in their visual field, including your torso. Thus, for maximum effect, choose the left lapel to display lapel pins or their equivalent.

Getting back to the formality of attire, take your cues from the group you are addressing. While a shirt and tie or other business attire may be perfectly appropriate when speaking before a Rotary Club, dressing down may be perfectly fine in other settings. But, be careful about presuming the appropriateness of attire.

Several years ago, when I was consulting for a major pharmaceutical company in the mid-western United States, I was invited to make a presentation at the company's retreat center in a rural area in Michigan. I arrived the night before and noted that all the attendees were dressed casually. I presumed that their dress signaled the likely attire for the session planned for the next morning. Imagine my surprise when I showed up in khaki pants and a polo shirt to give my first-scheduled presentation to an audience decked out in business attire. The experience was quite embarrassing and I took the opportunity at a late morning break to change clothes—in time for the company's chief operating officer to make his presentation. The take home message: always ask unless directions are clear.

So, you are properly attired for a speech or other presentation. You walk to your appointed speaking place with confidence and head erect. Next, comes the first greeting. A simple thank you or other polite acknowledgment for an introduction is in order, if you have been introduced properly. If not, make sure to announce who you are and why you are there. Then start with an honest comment about your pleasure at being with the group or note connections you may have with the group or its location. Avoid the commonly used "good morning routine" in which the speaker says loudly "good morning" anticipating a similarly loud and antiphonal "good morning" from the audience. Worst yet, when the first "good morning response" is feeble, admonishing the audience to make the greeting again and sometimes a third or fourth time. Akin to Robinson (2000), I think it may be "the worst way to begin a speech."

Close seconds to the "worst way" include self-critical remarks ("I am really not a very good speaker." or "I get very nervous speaking before audiences."), bad or offensive jokes, and anonymous quotes.

More affective openings include simple statements of your pleasure in being invited, acknowledgments of connections to the audience, expressions of gratitude for the audience's presence if you have convened the meeting, or an appropriate self-deprecatory remark as noted in Section II.

If you have foreign language skills and are addressing a group of people who you know well, you might try a technique that Tom Rochon (Vice President for Academic Affairs at the University of St. Thomas in St. Paul, Minnesota) uses to heighten attention at the beginnings of talks. Without any prior comment, he begins speaking in a foreign language. After a sentence or two, he stops suddenly and notes in English, "I see some quizzed looks so I will continue my remarks in English." The preamble is greeted with hearty guffaws.

Having crafted a great beginning, you'll want to consider—empathizing with the audience—"what comes next?" Next, involves what I call the "bookends of the talk."

THE BOOKENDS

Every basic communications text or course suggests a strategy for writing or giving a speech that involves:

- Outlining for the audience what you are about to say
- Saying it
- Summarizing for the audience what you just said

It may sound trite but this basic advice works and it is worthy reminding ourselves of its value. In this scheme are the "bookends"—the outline and the summary, which are important components of most talks that are twenty minutes or more in length. Each of the bookends deserves at least one slide in a PowerPoint™ presentation and the "bookends" can be embellished with artwork or other introductory illustrations as noted in Section II. Parallel to the thematic melodies heard in the beginning and ends of music—from classic to movie music to rock—the bookends help reinforce the themes that were most important in your talk.

In her recent work on Fred Rogers (i.e., Mr. Rogers), Ellen Handler Spitz (2003) notes how Mr. Rogers would describe—at the beginning of each show—the events that were planned subsequently. Spitz comments further that such advance notice gave, "children a chance to prepare themselves and to experience an empowering sense of anticipation and mastery." In my experience, adult audiences are affected similarly, and further appreciate both the outline and summary bookends of presentations.

The "saying it" portion of the talk requires a best effort using the tools, materials, and other ideas proffered through Chapters 2 through 12.

This brings us to the "something extra."

LAGNIAPPE

In Cajun, *lagniappe* means "something extra" and goes back to open market days when a merchant would add just a little more than what was paid for to insure satisfaction; the thirteenth item making up the "baker's dozen"—would be an example. But the true origin goes back to Medieval France when cereal grains were sold by parceling out portions with a piece of cloth. Because some grains would inevitably stick to the cloth, the merchant would "throw in" a handful of grains into the final amount sold *pour le nappe* (for the cloth), which later became *lagniappe*. In the context of speeches and other presentations, the *lagniappe* is a short story or anecdote, intriguing references to art or music, or possibly a prop. When sharing the *lagniappe* with audiences I often preface it with a anecdote from my childhood.

Growing up in the forties and fifties in the metropolitan New York area, I commonly accompanied my mom on her rounds to the bakery, the fruit and vegetable store, and the butcher shop. During this ritual, it was common for shopkeepers to give a child a sampling of the shop's goods—a cookie, an apple, or a piece of baloney. I usually note—in contemporary settings—that I plan not to give out any "baloney" but would like to offer something delectable at the end of a talk—to help crystallize memories of the occasion.

Thus, the *lagniappe* may involve allusions to sartorial accessories, art works, or artifacts as noted in Chapter 9. The resulting effect is wonderful.

So, you have the makings of a talk. In the next section, we will consider the presentation conditions that will help make your masterpiece a hit with audiences.

Section Four

Making Presentations

Akin to multi-talented architects who plan and supervise the construction and renovation of buildings, there comes the day when the finished project can be described to an audience—be it a professional group or general audience. What a thrill! And, what an opportunity to show off the creative work that went into the project. This scenario mimics the point where we are now—having pre-planned a presentation, having surveyed and used various tools, and having crafted a talk that now offers the final joy of presentation. So, let's get on with the show.

Chapter Fourteen

Presentation Tips and Techniques

We've crafted a great beginning. We've got the talk. We've planned what to wear. We're ready—right? Not quite. We need to consider factors that could ruin most of our efforts. Let's also make sure that all that has been crafted—up to the present—has the chance for airing in glorious fashion.

To insure presentation success, we'll need to think about: (1) final contacts with the host organization, (2) timing of arrival at the venue, (3) setting up equipment, (4) demeanor, body language, and presentation techniques, (5) handling questions and comments, (6) graciously following up. We'll consider these topics separately and in order.

FINAL CONTACTS

Be alert for contacts from a representative of the host organization or group a day or two before your scheduled presentation. If she or he does not contact you—make the contact yourself.

Double-check the date, time, and precise location (including the room number) for the presentation. Ask if there are expectations of your being earlier than you would normally plan to be at the venue. Ask who will introduce you. Ask if they have a biographical sketch. If not, make sure they get one. An example of a biographical sketch suitable for introductions is given in Appendix 10. No more than one page of single-spaced typed text is desirable.

Inquire about arrangements for equipment you will need for your talk. If the venue for the presentation is a restaurant or hotel, ask the contact person if he or she has assurances from the venue management relative to necessary equipment. So, now we are ready to plan an arrival.

TIMING OF ARRIVAL

Unless there are needs to the contrary, plan to arrive at the venue fifteen to thirty minutes before the presentation. This timing will permit opportunities for initial introductions and the setting up of equipment. The early arrival will also ease the "speaker appearance anxiety" that is often experienced among people who arrange presentations.

Ask who will introduce you and whether she or he has a copy of your biographical sketch. Of course, you will have brought along an extra copy of your biographical sketch to supplant one that may have been left behind.

During the pre-presentation chats, ask about the identity of those who may have recommended contact with you or who may have planned the program that included an invitation for you to speak. These folks deserve recognition during your opening remarks. Also, check to see if there are any dignitaries expected at the talk. If so, ask if your hosts would like for you to acknowledge their presence during your opening remarks. Be sure to save time to set up and check out your equipment.

SETTING UP EQUIPMENT

Always—and I mean always—try to bring your own projection equipment for a presentation. People are well meaning but you cannot count on hotels, restaurants, or for that matter—many other organizations and institutions to supply operable equipment and reliable technical advice for its use.

I can share horror stories about slides being put into slide trays upside down, slides being dumped on the floor during an attempt to correct a slide carousel malfunction, and a well-known San Francisco hotel that had to send a courier half-way across town for an adapter to connect a projector to a laptop computer. There are additional stories of overhead projectors with burnt out bulbs and hotel employees being unable to find a projector cart or projection screen, but there are some risks in life and you cannot rent a U-Haul truck to carry all the equipment you will need. The trick is to minimize risk and the best insurance involves—at minimum—bringing your laptop computer, projector, and props—as needed.

In addition to PowerPoint™ or other projection equipment, check out the microphone and sound system. As noted earlier, I prefer a portable or a lapel microphone to permit mingling with the audience during a presentation. Make sure the microphone and system work to your satisfaction. Particularly when using a lapel microphone, be sure that other microphones positioned at the podium or in the isles are turned off lest your audience experience deafening or annoying feedback.

After checking the projection of a slide image for visibility throughout the room, double-checking your laser pointer and slide advance system, and running through the slides for detection of possible last minute glitches—you should be ready to begin. One final thought, however, is to confirm with your host the expectation for length of your presentation. Now you are ready to go.

DEMEANOR, BODY LANGUAGE, AND PRESENTATION TECHNIQUES

You always hope that your introduction is appropriate and reasonably fair so the audience knows who you are and the background that makes you qualified to speak. Introductions run the gamut from awful to glowing. If the latter, be sure to humbly acknowledge the generous introduction.

Sometimes there are mistakes made during the introduction. Minor errors need not be corrected to avoid embarrassing your host. However, I do hold the line on references that may attribute false accomplishments or titles. Such mistakes should be politely corrected—before starting your speech—to set the record straight.

For many people—even those with considerable experience—giving presentations is difficult. The presentations—in turn—may appear stiff and uninspiring. Becoming a more effective and relaxed speaker is a challenge. But, the best seemingly paradoxical corrective advice is to reach a state where you "make it look easy." If you think about it, the most inspiring and effective speakers seem to practice their craft with ease.

One help with relaxation is breathing exercises. If it is not your practice already, consider while you are being introduced, taking several deep breaths through your nose and exhaling slowly (5–10 seconds) through your mouth.

Another aid is to simply give enough speeches that you build self-confidence. Additionally, you need to take heart in the notion that "no one knows what you are going to say, so if you leave something out or make a little mistake—few will notice."

More often than not, with practice, your level of relaxation will increase once you get into the early stages of the talk. Personally, once I am into the first 10–20% of a talk, a level of positive and pleasurable excitement sets in. I seem to float to a new plane where anxieties disappear. The words and actions seem to flow spontaneously.

Speaker competence and satisfaction are assisted by reactions from audience members. You see it in their eyes and in their expressions. You hear it through laughter and other expressions of joy. Accordingly, seek out these signs of acceptance—as you speak.

As you proceed through a talk, look for empathetic eyes among audience members. Establish eye contact—one-by-one—with these people. Seek eye contact with individuals scattered throughout the audience, dwelling no more than a few seconds with any single person.

From your earlier contacts with your hosts and participants you should have learned the names of some audience members. If you can meaningfully allude to these individuals during your talk, the allusions augment the bonds built through eye contact and other dramatic and intriguing elements crafted into the talk.

The audience interactions will help you achieve a level of joy that is highly motivating. Indeed, when you reach the plane of joy noted earlier, you will begin demonstrating the kind of enthusiasm that all great speakers display. The enthusiasm will be detectable through the variations in your voice, the gestures of your hands and arms, the look of your eyes, and the smile on your face. And, enthusiastic expression—often interpreted dramatically—should be accentuated the larger the audience (Detz 1992).

Even though you may achieve a level of ecstasy, watch the time carefully during your presentation. If you forget to check your wristwatch, anticipate clues from your host or chairperson for the session. Rising motions or worried glances are signals that time is expiring. Also respect timing lights or buzzers that may be used at venues such as scientific conferences.

At talk's end, you should be beaming—assuming all goes well, which is likely given your preparation and attention to detail.

O.K., you've ended the formal talk with a summary and offered the lagniappe (*e.g.*, ties that bind). It is now time to solicit questions and comments.

HANDLING QUESTIONS AND COMMENTS

After thanking the audience for their attention, indicate a willingness to answer questions immediately—unless your hosts have made other arrangements for Q and A. Repeat questions posed by members of the audience; then answer them honestly and succinctly. If you don't know the answer to a question respond forthrightly.

Sometimes, listeners become emotional about points raised during talks. In most instances, you need only to wait out the rhetoric and move on. Criticism, after all, can be taken in the spirit of free inquiry. Occasionally, however, a questioner displays poor manners and may become personally abusive. This is uncalled for and should be addressed properly by your meeting hosts. If not, a statement about the impropriety of a remark should suffice.

After the question-and-answer period, thank the audience and your hosts and return to your seat. Enjoy the exhilaration of having successfully completed a presentation.

If your talk represents the end of a program or if you need to wait for others to complete their speeches, it will be appreciated by your hosts if you stay a few minutes afterwards.

GRACIOUSLY FOLLOWING-UP

Being a gracious presenter includes staying a few minutes after your talk to greet members of the audience who may have additional comments to share or questions to ask. Be sensitive to this follow-up responsibility and be open to requests for additional written materials or references. I do ask petitioners, however, to send an e-mail note reminding me of their request and I provide them with a business card to facilitate the task. Accordingly, I always make sure to have an ample supply of business cards with me.

If the inquiring person takes the time to send a note I try to accommodate their requests as much as I am able. By asking for the follow-up note, you can screen for frivolous inquiries.

So, that's it. We've done it. We pre-planned, surveyed tools and materials, crafted the talk, and made the presentation in grand style. Some epilogue thoughts follow on what a passion for dramatic and intriguing presentations may mean to your professional and personal development.

Epilogue

Crafting and giving presentations represents one of the loves of my life. I hope this book personifies such passion. I hope as well, that I may have offered inspiration for professionals—as beleaguered as we feel at times—that the time spent crafting and giving presentations has special rewards both professionally and personally. Indeed, there is probably no better way to organize your thoughts and understanding of a topic than to write and speak about it. Great teachers know this well and it is one reason why people talk about a passion for teaching.

There are other personal and professional advantages to becoming first-class at crafting and presenting speeches. For one, crafting a speech is akin to outlining or writing an article for publication. The better you become at both—the more successful you will be. Also, like writing, speechmaking helps you find a "signature" to your personality and professional creativity. In varying places where I have worked, people call me the "tie man" because of my signature use of neckties to make points during talks. When I walk into a room where I am about to speak and there are people present who know me, one or more will come up, look at my necktie and ask, "How is that necktie going to be woven into your remarks today?" My typical response is—"You'll see." And so, the mystery, the drama, and the mystique grow in parallel to your reputation as a dramatic and intriguing speaker.

After developing a signature and a reputation for good speaking, opportunities for speechmaking will increase—to the benefit of the firm, institution, organization, or cause you represent. Thus, the time you spend in developing speechmaking skills should pay dividends—for your firm, institution, or organization—and you. The personal and professional benefits will be particularly manifest during times in your career when you need or wish to interview for a new and possibly more responsible position.

Some folks accuse me of not be able to hold a job since I have worked at five public research universities during my career. My retort is that it has taken more than thirty-five years to establish the record so the average is not all that bad. But, speaking abilities have been immensely important in being afforded the opportunities to make calculated moves during my career.

Through this book, I have now given up most of my best secrets to speech-making success. May they be as useful to you as they have been for me! *Bonne chance*.

Appendix One

Self-Deprecatory Humor

Lead in . . .

Humorous Comment or Reference

About humility necessary to be a successful manager or administrator . . .

I've learned through the years that there is some truth to the cynical old saw that "one half of the people in your organization think they could do the job better than you—the other half believe that *anyone* could do it better than you."

Or, As Benjamin Franklin (1706–1790) noted (Poor Richard's Almanac) many years ago: "A learned Blockhead is a greater Blockhead than an ignorant one." I have taken his advice seriously—throughout my life.

About organizational affiliations . . .

I have belonged to organizations that have been at the crossroads so long they should have been arrested for loitering.

When you speak about crossroads, you may also wish to refer to Woody Allen's sardonic quip: "More than any time in history, mankind faces a crossroad. One path leads to despair and utter hopelessness. The other road leads to extinction. Let us hope we have the wisdom to choose correctly." (Allen 1977)

About passing from this life . . .

They say that you ought not tell jokes at a funeral but here is one I adopted from Mort Sahl and used for a dear friend who I know would have appreciated it: "They say such wonderful things at your funeral and you miss it all. And, only by a few days!"

About a professional failure including speaking before audiences . . .

When I fear failure greatly, I take heart in a permutation of something known as Carson's Consolation, that is, "There are no complete failures, because people who fail can always be used as bad examples."

And, of course one of the great fears of failure is that connected with public speaking. Here's how this may be used: "They say that there are two great fears among Americans: First is the fear of speaking before an audience; the second is death!"

About professional success . . .

I like what Woody Allen says about professional success: "Half of life's success is showing up. The other half is being on time."

About retiring at age sixty-five . . .

I've been told that I should consider retirement at age sixty-five but I sometimes feel like American comedian George Burns (Nathan Birnbaum; 1896-1996) who used to quip that "Retirement at sixty-five is ridiculous. When I was sixty-five, I still had pimples."

And, when you contemplate retirement you think about retirement income, which triggers a recollection of Jackie Mason's comment: "I have enough money to last me the rest of my life, unless I buy something."

About seniors . . .

I have often been intrigued by how actress Mary Martin viewed advancing age when she said: "One of the worst irritations in life is the fact that by the time you get it all together, you're too old to lift it."

And, of course as I get older, I am sobered by baseball great Casey Stengel's observation: "Most people my age are dead."

About taking one's position too seriously . . .

When tempted to imagine how important I am—because of my position—I think of the admonishment of former U.S. Senator David Pryor who notes: "It takes six weeks to go from *Who's Who* to Who's He!"

I appreciate feedback but know realistically that it may not always be favorable. Although, perhaps not as critical as that of a message once received by Maurice Sendak, the author and illustrator of *Where the Wild Things Are* and many other children's books.

"Dear Maurice,
Your writing is stupid. I hope you die soon.
Cordially, Sylvia"

When I am tempted to take myself too seriously, I remember the old aphorism: "Administrators may be necessary, but they are certainly not important."

About your hobbies . . .

I used to really appreciate my talents, then I took up golf.

About your professional career . . .

I have worked at five research universities. Some people say I can't hold a job. But, the average tenure for each has been nearly seven years, so it's not so bad. (There are many permutations on this set of quips even for professionals younger than the author.)

About your professional position . . .

At one time I couldn't even spell pharmacist (or archeologist, actuary, or podiatrist), now I *are* one.

After receiving a highly complimentary introduction prior to giving a talk . . .

That introduction was a whole lot better than ones I have received when speaking in some of the remote corners of my state, where closing introductory comments have included the comment: "Now, we'll hear the dope from the University of Arkansas."

I recently noted the following tee shirt slogan: "I ran out of sick leave so I called in dead." After hearing that great introduction, I am happy that no one called me in "dead" today.

As guest of honor at an event . . .

I feel somewhat like Groucho Marx when he attended a party to commemorate his eighty-fifth birthday, "This can't be much of a party if I'm the guest of honor. I may leave early."

Appendix Two

Art and Artist References in the Talk: Art and Science of Personnel Development and Productivity in the Twenty-first Century Workplace

Slide Text

Artist (Nationality, lifespan dates), Art Work (year or years produced), Current Location of Art Work: Use in Talk and Art History References

Art Work(s): URL(s)

Presentation Outline: (1) The Twenty-first Century Workplace, (2) Personnel Development, (3) Productivity

Mark Rothko (American, 1903–1970), *No. 10* (1950), Museum of Modern Art, New York, N.Y.: The block-like work of Mark Rothko's *No. 10* symbolizes the four elements of the Presentation Outline slide and serves as an introduction to the talk by drawing upon the observation that Rothko wished to have his works displayed so they could be viewed up-close and with the thought of possibly passing through them as one might enter a portal (Rothko 2003). Thus, Rothko's work introduces the notion that one is passing from the outline to the substantive portions of the talk in an intriguing and symbolic manner.

Art Work: <http://www.nga.gov/feature/rothko/classic2.html>

The Twenty-first Century Workplace: Individual *versus* Team Efforts

Michelangelo Merisi da Caravaggio (Italian, 1571–1610), *The Cardsharps* (*I Bari*) (*circa* 1594), Kimball Art Museum, Fort Worth, Tex. and Georges de La Tour (French, 1593–1652), *The Cheat with the Ace of Clubs* (*circa* 1620), Kimball Art Museum, Fort Worth, Tex.: Michelangelo Caravaggio's and George de la Tour's depictions of cardsharps and their accomplices duping innocent participants in group play offer interesting examples of the dark side of team efforts. Thus, points can be made about the importance of individual *versus* team efforts in the twenty-first century workplace but with the caveat that work in teams may bring out behavior that must be avoided. The art examples allow the point to be made—dramatically—that managers must be conscious of the petty jealousies or disagreements that may arise during group interactions—primarily to prevent their adverse effects on organizations.

Art Works: <http://www.kimbellart.org/database/index.cfm?detail=yes&ID=AP%201987.06> and <http://www.kimbellart.org/database/index.cfm?detail=yes&ID=AP%201981.06>

The Twenty-first Century Workplace: Diverse and Non-Hierarchical

Wassily Kandinsky (Russian/German/French, 1866–1944), *Composition VI* (*aka Flood*) (1913), State Hermitage Museum, St. Petersburg, Russia: The mixture of color and form in Kandinsky's painting may be used to symbolize the diverse and non-hierarchical nature of the twenty-first century workplace. Allusion can also be made to Kandinsdy's role in the founding (1913–1914) of the art avant-garde group, *Der Blaue Reiter* ("The Blue Rider") (McMullen 2001) and how the avant-garde of the early twentieth century merged into the mainstream years later—akin to the adoption of multicultural perspectives and non-hierarchical principles of management from the late twentieth century into the twenty-first century workplace.

Art Work: <http://www.hermitagemuseum.org/html_En/03/hm3_3_1_10c.html>

The Twenty-first Century Workplace: Teaching and Communication Skills

Winslow Homer (American, 1836–1910), *Blackboard* (1877), The National Gallery, Wash. D.C.: The teaching setting of this artwork is symbolic of the point that professionals in the twenty-first century workplace need good teaching and communication skills. The latter is obvious to managers and audience members from varying professional milieu. The need for teaching skills emanates from the concept that in an information technology intensive workplace we all become teachers and for that matter—students. We learn from one another daily about software and hardware updates, new state and federal regulations, audit findings, and many other more or less technical and complex matters. The painting contains the ambiguity of the woman at the blackboard. Is she teacher or student? Her body language suggests some angst as she muses over mathematical or geometrical concepts. The subject, the pose, the apparent tension, permit use of the tension breaking quip, "There will always be prayers in schools so long as there are math tests."

Art Work: <http://www.nga.gov/cgi-bin/pinfo?Object=70344+0+none>

The Twenty-first Century Workplace: Advanced Portals

Joseph Stella (Italian-born American, 1880–1956), *Metropolitan Port* (*circa* 1937), Smithsonian American Art Museum, Washington, D.C.: In the context of this talk, advanced portals can be summed up as follows: Imagine a website or its equivalent, customized to a given professional's needs—complete with links to on-line and targeted digitized resources located throughout the world. Imagine also, services that update the professional's advanced portal and provide notices automatically—about new resources and services. Sound too good to be true? Actually, there are librarians and other professionals who believe that we will see the development and use of advanced portals during the early part of the twenty-first century. The artwork allusion here is in part a play on words, but is also used to draw analogy between advanced practice in the modern professional's world and the recognized advanced nature of Joseph Stella's art—in his day. Stella was in love with New York City (Jaffe 1988). His *Metropolitan Port* probably refers to ports in Manhattan.

Art Work: <http://www.nmaa.si.edu/> (search "Joseph Stella" within this site)

The Twenty-first Century Workplace: Virtual Workplace

Edward Hopper (American, 1882–1967), *House by the Railroad* (1953), Museum of Modern Art, New York, N.Y. and *Nighthawks* (1942), Art Institute of Chicago, Chicago, Ill.: The lonely eeriness portrayed in Hopper's *House by the Railroad* and the *Nighthawks* serve as counterpoints to the enhanced use of telecommunications in the near future and the likely long-range future teleportation of imagery that will advance the virtual workplace in the twenty-first century. The resemblances of the house in the former work to the Victorian house (at Universal Studios) used in Alfred Hitchcock's famous movie, *Psycho*, offers a humorous reference. Additional reference to Sister Wendy Beckett's (2000) claim that the *Nighthawks* portrays Edward Hopper and his jealous wife Jo at the counter in an establishment (modeled after a restaurant on Greenwich Avenue in New York City) with no doors—provides an ironic twist that audiences enjoy learning.

Art Work: <http://www.artchive.com/artchive/H/hopper/house_by_rr.jpg .html> and <http://www.artchive.com/artchive/H/hopper/nighthwk.jpg.html>

Personnel Development: Intellectual and Social Development

John Frederick Peto (American, 1854–1907), *The Poor Man's Store* (1885), Museum of Fine Arts, Boston, Mass.: The remarks in the personnel development and productivity sections of the talk are pitched to staff personnel, managers, and administrators. For this slide (Intellectual and Social Development), the importance of conference, workshop and meeting attendance is stressed. The Peto painting offers a light moment when its *trompe l'oeil* image is examined with the audience's participation. The audience is asked to ponder momentarily on this storefront window, which resembles the one described in Nathaniel Hawthorne's *The House of the Seven Gables*. A close examination of the window ledge reveals that the *Poor Man's Store* is also a place for lodging and the tilted sign hanging from a nail on the window ledge displays the announcement, "GOOD BOARD $3.00–week." A wry comment can then be offered about how managers would welcome such economy in our time. One can also note that Peto—a native Philadelphian—was never famous in his own time and relate how managers should be concerned about professional development, lest personnel pass on—in a mortal and figurative sense—without suitable opportunities.

Art Work: <http://www.mfa.org/handbook/portrait.asp?id=339&s=1>

Personnel Development: Continuing Education

Pablo Picasso (Spanish, 1881–1973), *Girl Reading at a Table* (1934), Metropolitan Museum of Art, New York, N.Y.: Continuing education (CE) is principally the responsibility of individuals—be they staff or management. However, staff and management should not only be supportive of CE, but also committed to finding innovative ways to meet mutually defined objectives. In this slide, the need for innovation in CE is symbolized through Pablo Picasso's *Girl Reading at a Table* and the narrative draws upon a known feature of the cubist art form. Specifically, we observe in Picasso's work, the cubist's attempt to portray in two dimensions, the three-dimensional elements of a subject—particularly elements that are not normally in the viewer's grasp. Cubism, therefore, symbolizes the innovation that managers and staff need to incorporate into CE plans. The symbolism provides a more interesting way of expressing the ideas imbedded in the terribly over-used phrase, "thinking outside of the box."

Art Work: < http://www.metmuseum.org/special/paris_painter/ma1996.403.1.R.htm>

Personnel Development: Professional Organizational Involvement

Pierre-Auguste Renoir (French, 1841–1919), *The Luncheon of the Boating Party* (1880–1881), The Phillips Collection, Washington, D.C.: Good managers recognize the value of professional organizational involvement. It can also be suggested that outstanding staff are those who not only participate but also earn leadership positions in professional organizations. The leadership efforts, which are typically donated unselfishly, provide professional growth opportunities that are often unparalleled in career development. The Renoir work offers the symbolism of the myriad benefits of professional organizational involvement and is symbolized by the different attitudes and interactions of Renoir's subjects during their luncheon outing.

Art Work: <http://www.phillipscollection.org/html/lbp.html>

Personnel Development: Mentoring

Louis-Léopold Boilly (French, 11761–1845), *The Geography Lesson* (1812), Kimball Art Museum, Fort Worth, Tex.: When Odysseus left on his fateful twenty-year journey to the Trojan wars (Homer *circa* 900–800 B.C.E.), he left his son, Telamachos, in the hands of the trusted advisor and guide—Mentor. In recent times, mentors have come to mean advisors or confidantes (men and women) "who make a difference" in the lives of students and professionals. The idea of mentoring is symbolized in this slide by the Boilly painting, *The Geography Lesson*. Created during the height of Napoleon's early nineteenth century battle with Russia, the painting portrays Monsieur Guadry, a French civil servant, providing a historical geography lesson to his daughter (Kimball Art Museum 2003). The beauty and poignancy of the Boilly painting helps make the point about the personalized nature of effective mentoring.

Art Work: <http://www.kimbellart.org/database/index.cfm?detail=yes&ID=AP%201990.01>

Personnel Development: Managerial Involvement

Grant Wood (American, 1891–1942), *American Gothic* (1930), Art Institute of Chicago, Chicago, Ill.: Whether as mentor or supervisor—or both—balanced and thoughtful managerial involvement in personnel development is obligatory to strong organizations and organizations with notable *esprit d'corps*. This sober advice is accentuated with the subtle humor embodied in Grant Wood's masterpiece and one of the world's best known paintings, *American Gothic*. Few people know that the models for the farmer and his spinster daughter are the unmarried sister of Grant Wood (*i.e.*, Nan Wood) and the artist's and his sister's dentist (Dr. Mckeeby) (Art Institute of Chicago 2003). One cannot resist the humorous and incongruous association of a pitchfork (literally in the right hand of the farmer and figuratively in the pattern of the bib of the farmer's overalls) and the normal *modus operandi* of dentists. Likewise the sour expression on the farmer's face provides a humorous reference to what personnel would rather not witness among supervisory managers.

Art Work: <http://www.artic.edu/aic/collections/modern/73mac_wood.html>

Productivity: Facilitating Routine Tasks

Pierre Puvis de Chavannes (French, 1824–1898), *Work* (c. 1863), The National Gallery, Washington, D.C.: Moving from personnel development to productivity, this first slide on facilitating routine tasks is illustrated by a copy of a painting that is simply titled, *Le Travail* or *Work*. Good managers know that efficiency is improved if routine tasks are facilitated—or eliminated. Engaging professional staff in the facilitation of routine tasks is also a sign of good management. This rather prosaic message is enlivened by the representation of a painting by the famous French fresco-like painter, Pierre Puvis de Chavannes. It is also fun to reflect on the double entendre embedded in the comparison between the French word for work, *le travail*, and the connotation of anguish commonly implied when using the English equivalent of "travail."

Art Work: <http://www.nga.gov/cgi-bin/pinfo?Object=1197+0+none>

Productivity: Innovation in All Efforts

Salvador Dali (Spanish, 1904–1989) *Lobster Telephone* (1936), Tate Britain, London: Imbuing innovation in all efforts is important for managers and staff professionals alike. But, there is an important reminder that parallel to U.S. patent law, innovation can only be adopted when it is both useful and is readily reduced to practice. The counterpoint to this argument, of course, and one found frequently in the art world is that creativity is encouraged without practical purpose. Although, the *Lobster Telephone* sculpture used in this slide, for example, can be humorously referred to as a communication device that comes with lunch. One can also take the opportunity to allude to an innovative use of Dali art in the well-known 1945 Alfred Hitchcock film, *Spellbound* starring Gregory Peck and Ingrid Bergman. In the film, Hitchcock used Dali's famous "melting clocks" and other *objets d'art* in dream sequences to illustrate the hero's attempts to escape psychological trauma.

Art Work: <http://www.tate.org.uk/servlet/AWork?id=2988>

Productivity: Cross-Training

Alberto Giacometti (Swiss, 1901–1966), *The Chariot* (1950), The Nelson-Atkins Museum of Art, Kansas City, Mo.: Productivity in the workplace is enhanced and sustained when professional staff are engaged in cross-training. Thus, at times of employee illness or other circumstances that take staff away from their posts—colleagues can fill in. These points are exemplified by Giacometti's sculptures which typically combine elements from different historic and social settings. *The Chariot*, for example, contains diverse elements that are allegedly traced back to an Etruscan incense burner, an 18th Dynasty Egyptian battle chariot, and perhaps a hospital pharmacy drug cart (Nelson-Atkins Museum of Art 2003).

Art Work: <http://www.nelson-atkins.org/collections/20thcent/detail/chariot.htm>

Productivity: Strategic Planning

Roy Lichtenstein (American, 1923–1997), *Blam* (1962), Yale University Art Gallery, New Haven, Conn.: The substance and process of strategic planning are vital to all organizations. Having staff buy into a common understanding of visions, missions, and sets of goals as well as specific objectives, have powerfully positive effects on organizations. The term "strategic planning" often conjures up the image of a military perspective and this association is played upon in the choice of the Roy Lichtenstein's *Blam* to illustrate this slide. Audiences are fond of learning that following his formal education at Ohio State University, Lichtenstein struggled to find a signature artistic style, until one day, a young son held up a comic book containing an image of Mickey Mouse and challenged his dad, "I bet you can't paint as good as that." Of course he could and so emerged his signature style of paintings containing photoengraver's Ben-Day dots, lettering, and speech balloons (Artchive 2003). During his career, portrayals of scenes from famous comic strips, including "Terry and the Pirates," and those embodying other military themes became prominent parts of Lichtenstein's lifelong portfolio.

Art Work: <http://www.artchive.com/artchive/L/lichtenstein/lichtenstein_blam.html>

Productivity: Quality Control and Quality Assurance

Max M. Autrey (American, dates unknown), Charlie Chaplin, *Modern Times* (1936), Motion Picture and Television Photo Archive, Los Angeles, Calif.: The terms, quality control (QC) and quality assurance (QA) in manufacturing industries, relate—in the first instance to standards of manufacturing and in the second instance—to insuring quality by independent surveillance. These terms are also applicable to a variety of management situations. In higher education, for example, standards are set by faculties for admission, matriculation, and graduation of students, and for curricula. Assessments of whether standards are being met come under the purview of institutional administrators and accrediting bodies. These and other examples help to make the point that QC and QA activities have significant influences on productivity—in a variety of organizations. The photos from the Charlie Chaplin film, *Modern Times*, are used as comic illustrations of the concepts portrayed through this slide. One can also point out the irony of this film allusion by noting how *Modern Times* was—for Chaplin—representative of protests of the introduction of sound into movies and in the larger context, the potentially negative impact of technology on society (Clooney 2002).

Art Works: <http://www.mptv.net/main/main_elements/mainpage.htm> (search "Modern Times" within this site)

Summary and Q/A

Thomas Cole (American, 1801–1848) *The Voyage of Life: Childhood*, *Youth*, *Manhood*, and *Old Age* (1842), The National Gallery, Washington, D.C.: The major points of the talk are considered in summary, namely the attempt to characterize the twenty-first century workplace, to present current personnel development features of that workplace, and to enumerate and illustrate factors that enhance productivity. In some ways, the talk represents a picture of modern professional life. Here, I offer a personal story of my early professional life, which included a side trip to the National Gallery while attending a professional conference in Washington, D.C. It was during that side trip that I was introduced to the great set of Thomas Cole paintings used to illustrate this slide. For some art historians, the paintings portray imagery of humankind—from birth to death—with a distinct emphasis on Christian beliefs. Other art historians believe that Cole was portraying the life and trials of his native country—America (National Gallery 2003). Whatever Cole's intend, his paintings provide a beautiful and interesting backdrop to a slide meant to help summarize the points in the talk and the finale of the presentation—in a dramatic and intriguing manner. As Cole once remarked, "I do feel that I am not merely a leaf painter." Indeed!

Art Works: <http://www.nga.gov/cgi-bin/pinfo?Object=52167+0+none>

Appendix Three

Quotes

Key Words or Context for Use

Quote. Author (lifespan dates). Biographical and Background Information. Source.

Criticism, Future, and Success

"I erase as I go along . . . I look forward so much I have only an imperfect memory for the past. When your eyes are directed to the future, you have no hurt feelings over the praises or criticism of the moment—because, moment by moment, the present becomes past. You have the sense of forever beginning your career, of trying to offer something new to interest the community."

Thorton Wilder (1897–1975). Seventeen years before he died, this three-time Pulitzer Prize-winning author (1928, *The Bridge of San Luis Rey*, 1938, *Our Town*, and 1943, *The Skin of Our Teeth*) offered the above thoughts in an interview.

"The human race has always wanted to control the future, or at least to predict what will happen."

Stephen Hawking (1942–). One of the greatest mathematicians and theoretical physicists of all time and a sufferer of amyotrophic lateral sclerosis (ALS or Lou Gehrig's Disease) since the early sixties, Hawking is Lucasian Professor of Mathematics at Cambridge University in the United Kingdom. His books, *A Brief History of Time* (1988) and *The Universe in a Nutshell* (2001), written for lay audiences, are world-wide bestsellers. The quote is from the latter book.

Dedication, Persistence, Freedom, and Perspective

"I have walked that long road to freedom. I have tried not to falter; I have made missteps along the way. But I have discovered the secret that after climbing a great hill, one only finds that there are many more hills to climb. I have taken a moment here to rest, to steal a view of the glorious vista that surrounds me, to look back on the distance I have come. But I can rest only for a moment, for with freedom come responsibilities, and I dare not linger, for my long walk is not yet ended."

Nelson R. Mandela (1918–). Civil rights leader and former President of South Africa, Mandela was a key leader in an effort—including twenty-seven years of imprisonment and house arrest—that led to the downfall of apartheid in South Africa. The quote is from *Long Walk to Freedom—The Autobiography of Nelson Mandela* (1995).

Education and Solving Problems

"Many of the problems facing us may be soluble, but only if we are willing to embrace brilliant, daring and complex solutions. Such solutions require brilliant, daring and complex people."

Carl Sagan (1934–1996). Former David Duncan Professor of Astronomy and Space Studies at Cornell University, Pulitzer Prize winner (*Dragons of Eden*), and one of the great contributors to the popular understanding of science in the twentieth century. Author and creator of the *Cosmos* series, which was viewed by more than five-hundred million people in sixty countries, Sagan also had a rare ability to probe human emotions and evoke thoughts of better worlds—to come. The quote is from *Broca's Brain* (1974).

"Education is the great engine of personal development. It is through education that the daughter of a peasant can become a doctor, that the son of a mineworker can become the head of the mine, that a child of farmworkers can become the president of a great nation. It is what we make out of what we have, not what we are given, that separates one person from another."

Nelson R. Mandela (1918–). See notes above.

Friendship and Love

"When one finds a person who has the same thought as yours, you cry out for joy, you go and shake him by the hand. Your heart leaps as though you were walking in a street in a foreign land and you heard your own language spoken, or your name in a room full of strangers."

Anne Morrow Lindbergh (1906–2001). Prize-winning author, wife, and co-pilot to Charles Lindbergh, Morrow Lindbergh wrote the above words in her diary (Berg 1998) soon after meeting and possibly falling in love with Antoine de Saint-Exupéry in 1939.

"For small creatures such as we the vastness [of the universe] is only bearable through love."

Carl Sagan (1934–1996). See notes above. The quote is from Sagan's novel, *Contact* (1985).

Goals and Life

"We are a culture of goal seekers. I have news for you—it's not the goal, it's the *trip* that's life. Life is the trip . . . life is getting there."

Leo F. Buscaglia (1924–1998). Fondly referred to as "Dr. Love," Buscaglia was a long-time faculty member at the University of Southern California (USC). He was well known for his course on "love" at USC and his endearing lectures—many of which that were broadcast on television, are now available through audio and videotapes. The quote is from *Living, Loving & Learning* (1982).

"According to the old saying, it is better to travel hopefully than to arrive."

Stephen Hawking (1942–). See notes and reference above.

Human Accomplishments and Teamwork

"The magic spirit of willing men . . . accomplishes more than the might of money or the marvels of machinery."

Rufus Woods (1878–1950). A giant of a man, Rufus Woods, through his work as editor and publisher of the *Wenatchee World* (Washington State), did more than any other person to inspire and cajole the federal government into building the Grand Coulee Dam in the thirties. In a commencement address to the 1942 graduating class of Grand Coulee High School, he offered his words of awe at the accomplishments of mortals—when they work together.

Interdisciplinary Studies

There are those "who straddle worlds and make of that very experience a new world."

Robert Coles (1929–). Eminent child psychiatrist and Pulitzer prize winning author (e.g., *The Call of Stories: Teaching and the Moral Imagination*, 1989), Robert Coles' abilities to "straddle the worlds" of medicine, literature, history, and music are well known. The quote is from an article by Grunwald (1985).

Learning

"Learning is the greatest joy. To learn something is fantastic because every time you learn something you become something new."

"The best way to love life is to love many things."

Leo F. Buscaglia (1924–1998). See notes and reference above.

"Happiness comes only when we push our brains and hearts to the farthest reaches of which we are capable . . . The purpose of life is to matter—to count, to stand for something, to have it make some difference that we lived at all."

Leo Rosten (1908–1997). Writer and social critic, who "made a difference" in adoption of Yiddish in American English, through works such as his 1968 book *The Joys of Yiddish*. The quote appears in Buscaglia (1982).

"As an academic diagnostician I would like to prescribe three remedies as a possible corrective to the illnesses of excessive specialization, humanistic isolationism, an enfeebled emotional life, and spiritual starvation. These are: (1) continuing education; (2) the reading of seminal books; and (3) the development of an interdisciplinary attitude toward science."

Blaise Opulente (1913–1983). English professor and university administrator, Opulente spent his academic career at St. John's University in New York. These words of advice were offered to an assemblage of pharmacy students about the time of my experience as an undergraduate at that memorable institution. I have often returned to "Opulente's Prescriptions" in writings and speeches prepared and delivered at a variety of venues.

"'The best thing for being sad,' replied Merlyn, beginning to puff and blow, 'is to learn something. That is the only thing that never fails. You may grow old and trembling in your anatomies, you may lie awake at night listening to the disorder of your veins, you may miss your only love, you may see the world about you devastated by evil lunatics, or know your honor trampled in the sewers of baser minds. There is only one thing for it then—to learn. Learn why the world wags and what wags it. That is the only thing which the mind can never exhaust, never alienate, never be tortured by, never fear or distrust, and never dream of regretting. '"

T(errence) H(anbury) White (1906–1964). A victim of an unhappy childhood and adolescence, White began to bloom in college and went on to write beloved fantasies, including the most famous tetralogy, *The Once and Future King* (1967). The latter book is the source of the quote.

Life and Living

"Oh God, to reach the point of death only to find that you have never lived at all."

"Spending . . . the best part of one's life earning money in order to enjoy a questionable liberty during the least valuable part of it, reminds me of the Englishman who went to India to make a fortune first, in order that he might return to England and live the life of a poet. He should have gone up garret at once."

"The mass of men lead lives of quiet desperation. What is called resignation is confirmed desperation."

"If men would steadily observe realities only, and not allow themselves to be deluded, life, to compare it with such things as we know, would be like a fairy tale and the Arabian Nights' Entertainments."

Henry David Thoreau (1817–1962). Essayist, social critic, Tanscendentalist, and non-conformist, Thoreau and his works are worth revisiting many times during one's life. His most famous work, *Walden*, was developed from a journal kept during 1845–1847 in a cabin near Walden Pond in Eastern Massachusetts, two miles south of Concord. Here, he grew his own food, observed, and wrote about life and nature—human and wild. While his cabin and its setting were intended to provide a Spartan existence for reflection, literary historians believe that Thoreau was treated to freshly baked pies and perhaps others goodies provided by nearby friends during his "survivalist adventure." The quotes are all from *Walden* (1854).

Mortality and Nature

"Every spring in the wet meadows and ditches I hear a little shrilling chorus which sounds for all the world like an endlessly reiterated 'We're here, we're here, we're here.' And so they are, as frogs, of course. Confident little fellows. I suspect that to some greater ear than ours, man's optimistic pronouncements about his role and destiny may make a similar little ringing sound that travels a small way out into the night."

Loren Eiseley (1907–1977). Anthropologist Eiseley served at different times as a faculty member at the University of Kansas, Oberlin College, and the University of Pennsylvania where he also served as Benjamin Franklin and University Professor of History and Science and Curator of Early Man in the University Museum of Archaeology and Anthropology. The quote is one of my all-time favorites and is from *The Immense Journey* (1957).

Retirement

"At the end, we think of the beginning."

Harold Rosen (1947–). Educator, philosopher, Unitarian-Universalist (U-U) minister, and currently Baha'i interfaith educator and organizer in Vancouver, British Columbia, Harold was born in New York City to a German Jewish father and Spanish Catholic mother, who he notes were both non-practicing, but respectful of their heritages. I love the quote and have used it many times to remind retirees that they are not their "position" in the institution they may have served for many years. In retirement talks, I also talk about how important it is to think about your roots and your "love-of-life" interests as you anticipate a major transition in life. For me, I collect lapel pins and neckties to remind myself of places where I have worked and lived. Wearing these sartorial accessories helps me revel in the enjoyable moments of the past. The quote comes from Harold Rosen's farewell sermon to the Moscow, Idaho U-U Fellowship (now the U-U Church of the Palouse) in 1987.

"Life is a distillation process, in which a year of experience yields a sometimes embarrassingly small amount of wisdom. As my professional career winds down—reaching perhaps a semicolon—I reflect on it as having been a profoundly enriching experience, one of rare and special privilege."

Sam C. Smith (1922–). Anticipating his retirement two years hence, Sam Smith, former Executive Director of the M. J. Murdock Charitable Trust in Vancouver, Washington, shared these insightful thoughts in a 1986 report published by the Murdock Trust. The allusion to the "semi-colon" as a metaphor for retirement or other transitions in life is fascinating. The humility reflected in the first sentence of the quote is also remarkable. Marian Haro (Executive Assistant to the Executive Director of the M. J. Murdock Charitable Trust) confirmed the quote in a telephone call in 2003 to Sam Smith.

"Age by itself does not bring wisdom, nor does youth automatically bring a fresh viewpoint: some individuals are born doctrinaire, and others embrace new ideas until the day they die."

Daniel E. Koshland, Jr. (1920–). Professor of the Graduate School of Biochemistry and Molecular Biology at the University of California Berkeley and former Editor of *Science*, these words were penned and published in a 1988 *Science* editorial titled, "Retire or Not to Retire, That Is the Question." While I try to avoid the common pitfall of equating retirement to mortal passing, this offers an inspirational thought worth sharing to prospective retirees.

Service to Humanity

"The more decisions you make in your life, the more times you act, the more certain it is that you will be wrong. To be fulfilled we need to recognize, all of us, that the world doesn't owe us a living—rather we owe the world a living. And in the brief time that is given us, we must somehow learn to give ourselves away."

"We are human because we care. All true meaning is shared meaning. The only thing that can never be taken from us is the love we give away."

F. Forrester Church (1948–). Son of Idaho's great twentieth century Senator, Frank Church, Forrester is Senior Minister at the All Soul's Unitarian Church in New York City. The first quote is taken from an article in *The World* (1988). The second quote comes from a sermon given by Rev. Church in the All Soul's Church on September 12, 2001.

Appendix Four

Proverbs*

African

"Nothing wipes your tears away but your own hand."
"There are three friends in this world: courage, sense, and insight."

American

"The things which hurt, instruct." Franklin (*circa* 1757)
"Time is an herb that cures all diseases."
"To be trusted is a greater compliment than to be loved." Franklin (*circa* 1757)

Chinese

"A bit of fragrance always clings to the hand that gives you roses."
"A journey of a thousand miles begins with but a single step."
"Deep doubts, deep wisdom; small doubts, little wisdom."
"Experience is a comb that nature gives us when we are bald."
"If you have two loaves of bread, sell one and buy a lily."
"If you wish to know the road ahead, inquire of those who have traveled it."
"The essence of a city is its people, not its walls."
"The person who says it cannot be done should not interrupt the person doing it."
"What I hear, I forget. What I see, I remember. And what I do, I understand."
"When things go wrong—look in the mirror."

---

* Proverbs with no citations are from *IdeaBank®* (see *Bibliography*).

Dutch

"Who gives to me, teaches me to give."

English

"May you live all the days of your life."
"One good head is better than a hundred strong hands."
"Something old, something new, something borrowed, something blue."

Ethiopian

"When the heart overflows, it comes out through the mouth."

German

"A bad reputation has better legs than a good one."

Greek

"All things good to know are difficult to learn."
"If it were not for hope, the heart would break."
"The excess of a virtue is a vice."

Hebrew

"Rivalry of scholars advances wisdom."

Irish

"Seldom is the last of anything better than the first."

Italian

"Be a voice, not an echo."
"Who stops learning grows old."

Japanese

"Fish die by the mouth."
"There are no national frontiers to learning."

Mexican

"He who doesn't look ahead stays behind." Detz (1992)

Norwegian

"Necessity teaches new arts."

Spanish

"You can have all the rest of the year if you will give me April and May."

Swedish

"Honor the house in which you were born, the tree that gave you shade, and the village in which you grew up."

Yugoslavian

"If you wish to know what a man is—place him in authority." (Perlman, 1998)

Appendix Five

Colors and Associated Disciplines, Symbolism, and Virtues*

Color

Associated Disciplines. Symbolism and Virtues.

Red

Allied Health, Family Studies (maroon), Natural Resources (russet or reddish brown).

Blood, courage, life-force, masculinity, passion, warmth; the Greek god of war, Mars and Roman god of war, Jupiter; in the Chinese culture, good luck; for practitioners of the Hindu *vastu* (*vastu shasta* or "abode knowledge") or the Chinese version—*feng shui* (pronounced "fong shway"), red is the color of the east and power.

Pink

Music, Public Health (salmon pink).

Breast cancer awareness and research, femininity, innocence, youth.

Orange

Engineering.
Healing.

---

*Academic references were adopted from the University of Connecticut Commencement Booklet (1999); several other references to mythology and art are from Fontana (1993) and Hornung and Bryan (2002); the references to vastu and *feng shui* are from Whelan (2002).

Apricot

Nursing.

Brown

Agriculture, Architecture, Fine Arts.
Earth, richness.

Yellow

Library Science (lemon), Social Work (citron or grayish green yellow).

Bright, cowardice, disease, humility, quarantine, sunny; for practitioners of *vastu* or *feng shui*, yellow is the color of the south or southeast and justice.

Yellowish-brown or drab

Business.

Gold

Science.

Immortality, inertness, permanence, reason, sun; associated with the Greek myth of Jason and the golden fleece.

Green

Medicine (forest), Pharmacy (olive).

Environment and environmental awareness, goodness, godliness, hope, jealousy, nature, vibrancy.

Blue

Education (light blue), Philosophy (dark blue).

Art, compassion, coolness, contemplation, depth, depression, faith, intellect, risqué, sky, truth, water, wisdom; the Greek goddess of love, Aphrodite and Roman goddess of love, Venus; in ancient Egyptian lore, blue was the color for rejuvenation as manifest in the paint used for the Ankh—or symbol for life; for practitioners of *vastu* or *feng shui*, blue is the color of the north and health and wealth.

Indigo

Public Administration.

Dark, death, harmony, rich, sorrow, underworld; according to Hindu belief, indigo or black is associated with time and the goddess of destruction, Kali;

in ancient Egypt, black was associated with rebirth and resurrection; for practitioners of *vastu* or *feng shui*, black is the color of the northeast, west or southwest and purity, prosperity, eating or feasting, or misery (take your pick!).

Violet

Dentistry (lilac), Law (purple).

Life, mourning, ornate, regal, royal, sorrow, truth; analogous to the discussion of the color, heliotrope (see Chapter 4), violet can be thought of as a combination of the "courage" of red and the "wisdom" of blue.

White

Arts and Letters.

Enlightenment, integrity, purity, transcendence, virginity; for practitioners of *vastu or feng shui*, white is the color of the northwest and economics and public relations.

Appendix Six

Historical Allusions and Quotes

Topic or Theme

Allusions, Quotes, and References

Ancient Civilizations, History of Western Thought,
Myth and Reality,
Migrations of Peoples Across the Earth

Ancient Greek thought, including mythology, provides rich references for practically any presentation. Many do not know that the ancient Greek myths embody elements of Greek history. Indeed, audiences will be intrigued to learn that it was not until the first archaeological digs at Mycenae (by the amateur archeologist Heinrich Schliemann [1822–1890]) in the middle nineteenth century (Cartledge 1998) that allusions to apparent historic references in the Homeric poems, the *Iliad* and the *Odyssey* (both *circa* 900–800 B.C.E.), were based on reality. Previously, few thought that these epic poems contained allusions to facts.

As indicated in Appendix 9, I have often employed allusions to the self-devouring serpent used to symbolize creation, re-creation, and the interrelatedness of all things. In Egyptian and Greek lore, the term for this creature is *Ouroboros* and it serves as a metaphor for the wonderful scholarly studies in history and the classics that have illuminated our understanding of ancient cultures, including those of ancient Greece.

Among the broad range of ancient historically illuminating literature, I have found fascinating the travels and writings of Thor Heyerdahl (1979, 1995, 2002), whose trip to Polynesia in the thirties led to a lifelong pursuit of an understanding of ancient humans and their travels. Through Heyerdahl's adventures, one can craft a chronology of civilization's development from Sumer to Egypt to the New World and the South Pacific, drawing upon real-life stories that tap into archetypal references to journeys and oceans. I have also used Jared Diamond's great Pulitzer Prize-winning book, *Guns, Germs, Steel* (1997) as a wonderful resource for information on the migration and development of societies around the globe.

Looking at more "modern societies"—that is, from the Renaissance to present day, requires careful assessment of economic and military power. Such assessments were well developed in Paul Kennedy's work, *The Rise and Fall of the Great Powers* (1987), in which he noted: "different regions and societies across the globe have experienced a faster or slower rate of growth, depending not only upon the shifting patterns of technology, production, and trade, but also upon their receptivity to the new modes of increasing output and wealth . . . the intellectual breakthrough from the time of Renaissance onward, boosted by the coming of the 'exact sciences' during the Enlightenment and Industrial Revolution, simply meant that the dynamics of change would be increasingly more powerful and self-sustaining than before." While Kennedy's treatise has less value for developments post 1987, it does serve as an excellent resource for information on economic and political development —world-wide. When coupled with allusions to the history and the evolution of philosophical thought, particularly Western thought, one can weave powerful ideas into presentations.

American Revolution, Founding Leaders, Patriotism, and the Early Political Landscape of the United States

Audience members are fascinated by the political factionalism that existed during Revolutionary times, especially the significant allegiance to the English Crown among many Americans.

Audiences also appreciate reminders about France being an ally to the young American Republic. Some audience members may be old enough to remember the flap that actress Jane Fonda caused with her comments to the contrary on late night television in the early seventies, relative to her opposition to America's involvement in Viet Nam. I also enjoy reminding audiences that the American Constitution is one of the oldest democratic documents on earth, along with its influence, as well as that of the American Revolution, on the French revolution, which climaxed in 1789.

Thomas Jefferson, his life and contributions to the United States make fascinating references. As indicated in Chapters 1 and 6, the story of Jefferson's commitments to the exploration of the West are intriguing, especially as they pertain to the quest for understanding in the natural sciences and humanities.

Audiences will also be fascinated by the picture Fawn Brodie (1974) paints of Jefferson—a man of self-doubt but great leadership skills—a highly organized and scholarly man—a man who wrote his own bible, among other works. These are all insights that intrigue audiences. Comments about Jefferson's brilliance are enhanced by an incident described by former Representative and Secretary of the Interior, Morris Udall (1988). The incident was a dinner hosted by President John F. Kennedy for Nobel Laureates on April 29, 1962, during which, Kennedy allegedly noted: "I think this is the most extraordinary collection of talent, of human knowledge, that has ever been gathered together at the White House, with the possible exception of when Thomas Jefferson dined alone."

Other founders of the United States provide captivating historic allusions. George Washington, gentleman farmer, astute warrior, Commander-in-Chief of the Revolutionary Army, and President of the Constitutional Convention of 1787, is best known, of course, as the first President of the United States—elected to this post in 1789. Washington was a self-effacing and reluctant but unstintingly dedicated and disciplined public servant. His prescience not only about America's frailties (esp. regional rivalries) but also the country's ultimate importance on the world stage (even though his only travel outside of the then Continental U.S. was to Barbados), are legendary. Washington's wishes for America were most notably stated in his *Farewell Address*, which was actually never given in public oration, but published in Philadelphia by the *American Daily Advertiser* on September 19, 1796. Audiences will be surprised by this fact and fascinated by quotes from the address. Alexander Hamilton drafted the *Farewell Address* but, according to historians (Nevis and Graff 2002), the work clearly contains expressions of Washington's philosophy and feelings for his beloved country. Who can question the humility of a man, having served as U. S. President for several years, proclaiming, "In the discharge of this trust (of the American people), I will only say that I have, with good intentions, contributed toward the organization and administration of the government the best exertions of which a very fallible judgment was capable." along with, "If benefits have resulted to our country from these services, let it always be remembered . . . (that) the constancy of your support was the essential prop of the efforts and a guarantee of the plans by which they were effected." And, what finer succinct expressions of patriotism and the power of union can there be than Washington's farewell assertions: "The name of American, which belongs to you, in your national capacity, must always exalt the just pride of patriotism more than any appellation derived from local discriminations . . . To the efficacy and permanency of your Union, a government for the whole is indispensable." Finally, his faith in the power of education and international good will are reflected in these farewell remarks: "Promote, then, as an object of primary importance, institutions for the general diffusion of knowledge. In proportion as the structure of a government gives force to public opinion, it is essential that public opinion should be enlightened." and "Observe good faith and justice toward all nations. Cultivate peace and harmony with all."

It bothers me that women are not represented significantly in the historic literature of the Revolutionary War period. Thus, I have often reflected on the following assertion, written by Abigail Adams in 1774 in a letter to her destined-to-be-President husband, John: "I long to hear that you have declared an independency . . . I desire you would remember the ladies . . . If particular care and attention is not paid to the ladies, we are determined to foment a rebellion and will not hold ourselves bound by any laws in which we have no voice or representation."

As a follow-up to a somewhat Americocentric view of the Revolution and the early social, economic, and political landscape of the United States, I am fond of quoting from Alexis de Tocqueville's *Democracy in America*, which was published in 1835 following an extended trip through the young Republic. His observations are uncanny for their insight and lasting quality. For example, consider his criticism of public speakers in America—criticism that is often valid today: "I have frequently noticed that the Americans, who generally treat of business in clear, plain language, devoid of all ornament and so extremely simple as to be often coarse, are apt to become inflated as soon as they attempt a more poetical diction. They then vent their pomposity from one end of a harangue to the other; and to hear them lavish imagery on every occasion, one might fancy that they never spoke of anything with simplicity."

History of the Smithsonian Institution and Roots of American Philanthropy

Audiences love the story of James Smithson and the founding of the Smithsonian Institution (the largest museum complex in the world) in Washington, D.C. This story also serves as a touchstone for allusions to American philanthropy.

Briefly, James Smithson (1765–1829)—the illegitimate son of Elizabeth Hungerford Keate Macie and Hugh Smithson (the first Duke of Northumberland)—was an Oxford-educated scientist who, following his death in Genoa, Italy, bequeathed $508,318 "to the United States of America, to found at Washington, under the name of the Smithsonian Institution, an establishment for the increase and diffusion of knowledge among men." The gift was not initially well thought of by the U.S. Congress and some other factions in the U.S. because of its "foreign roots" but was eventually accepted in a bold move by President Andrew Jackson in 1835. Three years later, the will was probated and funds transferred to the U.S. And, in 1855, the Smithsonian Museum (the so-called Castle—the red brick Victorian structure on the south side of the Mall in Washington, DC) was completed. Seventy-five years after James Smithson's death—in 1904—his remains and crypt were transferred to the Smithsonian through the efforts of Alexander Graham Bell who was then a Regent for the Institution. The crypt is maintained for public viewing in a chamber just to the left of the front lobby of the original museum building. I love to share the fact that I have visited this "mausoleum" many times to honor one of America's first philanthropists. I also like to leave audiences with the suggestion that James Smithson's dream represents the power of giving—figuratively and literally—in a particularly poignant manner.

I first became aware of the story of James Smithson from a book written by Virginia White (1975) (see Bibliography), but, you will find an expanded and illustrated version of this great tale on a website developed and maintained by the Smithsonian Institution. <http://www.sil.si.edu/Exhibitions/Smithson-to-Smithsonian/who_01.html>

American Civil War

Whether you live in the northern or southern half of the United States, you'll find great intrigue among Americans for references to the American Civil War. Indeed, I have found Civil War buffs in all eight states I have lived in from Northeast to the mid-West to the Pacific Northwest and the South. The fascination comes in part from the realization, for many, that the Civil War was America's most deadly war (with losses on both sides exceeding 600,000). Also, there is the recognition that the war was one of brother against brother and sister against sister, that it represented an extraordinary cancer relative to slavery in America, and that it was a war that could have literally destroyed the future of one of earth's great countries. Couple some of these ideas with the love and respect Americans have for their sixteenth President, Abraham Lincoln, and you have dynamite material to weave into many talks.

There are countless books and materials on the U.S. Civil War, but my Civil War historian colleagues, particularly James Swan, recommend those by Foote (1986), McPherson (1988), and Ward *et al.* (1990). And, don't forget that the U.S. Civil War was one of the first conflicts to be extensively photographed, thanks to the great work of New Yorker, Mathew Brady, and his colleagues. Many of Brady's photographs can be viewed at websites developed and maintained at the National Library of Congress <http://memory.loc.gov/ammem/cwphtml/cwbrady.html>, the National Portrait Galley <http://www.npg.si.edu/exh/brady/index.htm>, and Temple University <http://www.temple.edu/photo/photographers/brady/matt1.html>.

The Progressive Era and Social Movements of the Late Nineteenth and Early Twentieth Centuries

The post-Civil War period up through World War I was witness to a variety of social movements that provide wonderful allusions for talks. Consider a few examples: (1) The story of Harvey Washington Wiley (1844–1930) and the fight he and his colleagues waged through the U.S. Food and Drug Administration's precursor agency (the Division of Chemistry) against adulterated, contaminated, and misbranded foods and drugs, makes for inspiring historical allusions. Be sure to include allusion to the 1906 Pure Food and Drug Act, signed into law by President Theodore Roosevelt and memorialized as the "Wiley Act." Also, consider how important the 1906 law was to the later passage of the Food, Drug, and Cosmetic Act of 1938 (signed by President Franklin Delano Roosevelt), which dealt with drug safety as a result of the notorious sulfanilamide elixir case in which over one-hundred people died from a concoction containing anti-freeze (ethylene glycol) as a solvent for a poorly alcohol soluble drug (Kurian, 1998); (2) While women's right to vote was secured in the State of Wyoming in 1869, universal suffrage for women would have to wait until 1920 and the passage of the Nineteenth Amendment of the Constitution. The work in between was led by a host of familiar activists from Susan B. Anthony (1820–1906) to Elizabeth Cady Stanton (1815–1902) and her daughter Harriot Eaton Stanton Blatch (1856–1940) to Lucretia C. Mott (1793–1880), and Matilda Joslyn Gage (1826–1898), among many others (Flexner and Fitzpatrick, 1996). Stories of these brave and persistent women provide powerful and inspiring historical allusions, particularly for contemporary audiences whose members may take the efforts of American heroines for granted; (3) Jane Addams (1860–1935) also provides inspiring historical allusions, because of her birth into a wealthy family, her personal illness, the change in her life from travels in Europe, where she witnessed abject poverty, and her subsequent founding of what would become the most notable social work program in the world—Hull House (named after the builder Charles Hull). Addams recognition in later life—through her honorary degrees and the sharing of a Nobel Peace Prize (with Nicholas Murray Butler) in 1931 (Davis, 2000) are also reminders of the unselfishness of this great woman.

History of Aviation and the Adventures of Early Aviators

The history of modern aviation, approximately from the early twentieth century to World War II, offers adventuresome references for presentations. Starting with the lives of Orville and Wilbur Wright, originally bicycle builders in Dayton, Ohio, and continuing with successor pioneering efforts of aviators such as Charles Lindbergh, Anne Morrow Lindbergh, Wiley Post, Antoine St. Exupéry, and Amelia Earhart, one can draw upon rich and exciting tales to embellish talks. I am particularly fond of the legendary story of the Lindberghs, which blends scientific and technological challenges with personal pathos and the political naiveté of Charles Lindbergh—in complex but extraordinarily intriguing ways (Berg, 1998). The fact that Lindburgh, following his solo flight across the Atlantic in April of 1927, became the twentieth century's first celebrity (Berg, 1998), offers a source of dramatic and intriguing allusions, among many others related to early aviators and aviation.

World War II and the Subsequent Scientific Revolution in the United States

The profound economic, ethical, political, and social effects of World War II on the United States and the rest of the world, represent allusions I have used in many talks. As examples, you may wish to consider: (1) the decisive impact the war had on reversing America's stubborn depression; (2) the stupefying results of the Holocaust perpetuated by the Axis powers, not only against citizens of Jewish origin, but also gypsies and people with disabilities; (3) the evolution of America's foreign policy relative to the failings of fascism and communism; (4) the effects that World War II would ultimately have on social equality for women (remember "Rosie the Riveter") and minorities, the latter of whom would benefit in the sixties from Civil Rights Legislation that resulted in part from compelling arguments relative to the contradiction posed by outstanding service of our nation's minorities to the war effort on the one hand *versus* inequalities experienced in America following the war; (5) the beneficent character and strength of the American generation who lived through the war, as ably documented by Brokow (1998).

Finally, one of my favorite themes—based on talks I have given before many audiences—revolves about the effects that World War II had on America's role in scientific research through the end of the twentieth and now into the twenty-first centuries. Briefly, the United States was a third-rate player in scientific research until World War II presented challenges that American researchers from universities, federal laboratories, and industrial firms—often collaboratively—tackled skillfully. The threatened development of nuclear devices by the Nazis inspired teams of researchers at Princeton University, the University of Chicago, Los Alamos, and Hanford to conduct complex physical, chemical, and engineering research and development unlike anything previous.

When the Japanese cut off the Allies' supply of quinine, teams of biological, chemical, and clinical researchers organized to develop substitutes for the naturally-derived anti-malarial drug quinine. These projects, and others, affected the course of human history and helped to change completely the face of American scientific research.

America's newfound prowess continued after the war, due in part to the wisdom of President Roosevelt and President Truman's science adviser, Vannevar Bush, whose short though seminal 1945 report, *Science: The Endless Frontier*, set a precedent for federal support of research up to the present day (Zachary, 1997).

Bush argued that America should place its faith in basic or fundamental research and out of this would flow the necessary private investments for development and commercialization. The results of subsequent decades of research have contributed greatly to the current superpower status of the United States (Smith and George 1993 and 1994).

The American Civil Rights Movement

Most people have an awareness of the American Civil Rights movement and its heightened activities in the sixties, but few are aware of some of its historic roots. My involvement in a project between the University of Connecticut and the African National Congress (ANC) in South Africa made me aware of the international roots of the American movement—antecedents that audiences find fascinating.

People instantly recognize references to the "founder"—Mahatma Gandhi (born Mohandas Karamchand Gandhi)—of the Republic of India, but few know that as a man of twenty-five and in 1893, he went to South Africa to fulfill a one-year contract to practice law. That one-year would turn into twenty-one years of service to the Indian community in South Africa. During this two-decade long period, Gandhi would learn that persistence, good humor, reasoned thought, and the disarming of social enemies through acts of kindness, represented a powerful formula for effecting social change. Of course, it was this strategy that would eventually topple British rule in India (Nanda, 1992). But, it was also a behavior that inspired a strategy and belief system that would guide the efforts of Nelson Mandela in his so-called "Long Walk to Freedom" (Mandela, 1994). The ANC was not above violent acts but it was Mandela's Gandhi-like approach that turned the tide through twenty-seven years of imprisonment by the South African government. And, it was the example of Gandhi and Mandela that influenced greatly, Martin Luther King, Jr. and the Southern Christian Leadership Coalition, in their efforts to influence civil rights commitments and legislation in the United States. When alluding to the American Civil Rights movement, I find that the story of its "international roots" is perceived with significant drama and intrigue.

Appendix Seven

Literary Quotes, References, and Background

Topic or Theme

Quote. Reference. Author (lifespan dates). Biographical and Background Information.

Breakfast

"Life, within doors, has few pleasanter prospects than a neatly arranged and well-provisioned breakfast table." (Hawthorne 1851).

Nathaniel Hawthorne (1804–1864). Hawthorne was one of America's great nineteenth century authors. He was tortured by thoughts of the excesses of his Puritan ancestors, who included principals responsible for the Salem witch trials. Many of his thoughts (*i.e.*, particularly those noted below) reflect this mental agony but have a timelessness that make them ring true—more than one-hundred and fifty years since they were penned.

Death

"There's no understanding it. No understanding death. We all pretend we don't know it's coming. Then it's here. Doing this to us, tearing us apart, taking us back to nature." (Gilchrist 2000).

Ellen Gilchrist (1935–). Ellen Gilchrist is a noted Southern author who writes poignantly about people and places in the South; but her short poems, novels, and stories have universal appeal. Gilchrist lives on the Ozark Plateau in Fayetteville, Arkansas.

"It is very singular how the fact of a man's death often seems to give people a truer idea of his character, whether for good or evil, than they have ever possessed while he was living and acting among them. Death is so genuine a fact that it excludes falsehood, or betrays its emptiness; it is a touchstone that proves the gold, and dishonors the baser metal." (Hawthorne 1851).

Good Luck

"Not seldom in this life, when, on the right side, fortune's favorites sail close by us, we, though all adroop before, catch somewhat of the rushing breeze, and joyfully feel our bagging sails fill out." (Melville 1851).

Herman Melville (1819–1891). Melville's great novel, *Moby Dick*, is noted for its character development, its stunning prose, and its authenticity relative to the natural history of the sea. The story and characters offer great archetypal material.

Honoring and Remembering Friendship

"To forget a friend is sad. Not every one has had a friend. And if I forget him, I may become like the grown-ups who are no longer interested in anything but figures . . . said the little prince. 'I am looking for friends. What does that mean—tame?' 'if you tame me, [said the fox] then we shall need each other. To me, you will be unique in all the world. . . . if you tame me, it will be as if the sun came to shine on my life. I shall know the sound of a step that will be different from all the others. Other steps send me hurrying back underneath the ground. Yours will call me, like music, out of my burrow.'"

"'One runs the risk of weeping a little, if one lets himself be tamed.' . . . thought the Little Prince when leaving the fox."

"It is only with the heart that one can see right. What is essential is invisible to see." (Saint-Exupéry 1943).

Antoine de Saint-Exupéry (1900–1944). French aviator and celebrated author, Saint-Exupéry is particularly well known for the *The Little Prince*, which has sold more than fifty million copies in one-hundred and twenty languages. The power of *The Little Prince* is its poetic description of the relationships, eccentricities, foibles, and frailties of creatures—mythical and real.

Human Temperament

"There are people who derive extraordinary enjoyment from their sensitiveness, especially when it reaches a climax, as it very quickly does with them. At that moment I believe they would positively prefer to have been insulted rather than not. These irritable people are always horribly fretted by remorse afterwards, if they have sense, of course, and are capable of realizing that they have been ten times as excited as they need have been." (Dostoyevsky 1869).

Fyodor Dostoyevsky (1821–1881). One of Russia's great nineteenth century authors, Dostoyevsky presents sometimes confusing but nevertheless penetrating and timeless characterizations and comments on the ironies and ambiguities of human existence.

"[The] simplest division . . . of the human race is into the people who take things hard and the people who take them easy." (James 1886).

Henry James (1843–1916). A native New Yorker, born into a privileged family, lived and studied in Europe, but first blossomed as an author while studying and living in Cambridge and Boston, Massachusetts. Renowned in his own time, Henry James wrote many engaging and memorable magazine stories and novels.

Life and its Mixed Blessings

"If we look through all the heroic fortunes of mankind, we shall find this same entanglement of something mean and trivial with whatever is noblest in joy or sorrow. Life is made up of marble and mud." (Hawthorne 1851).

Life and Joy

"It's life that matters, nothing but life—the process of discovering, the everlasting and perpetual process, not the discovery itself, at all." (Dostoyevsky 1869).

"This is the true joy in life . . . being used for a purpose recognized by yourself as a mighty one . . . being thoroughly worn out before you are thrown on the scrap heap . . . being a force of Nature instead of a feverish selfish little clod of ailments and grievances complaining that the world will not devote itself to making you happy." (Shaw as quoted in Cook 1977).

George Bernard Shaw (1856–1950). Shaw was born in Dublin but acclaimed as a great English critic, essayist, journalist, novelist, and most especially, playwright. He is probably best known in the United States for his 1914 play, *Pygmalion*, which became the basis for the smash Lerner and Lowe musical, *My Fair Lady*, first produced on Broadway in 1956 and later immortalized by Rex Harrison and Audrey Hepburn who starred in the film of the same name.

Love

"Love changes everything.

Now I tremble at your name.

Nothing in the world will ever be the same." (Webber 1990).

Andrew Lloyd Webber (1948–). British author, composer, and producer, Webber has made great contributions to contemporary musical theater throughout the world. Probably best known in the United States for his Antoinette Perry Awards (Tony Awards) for the best musicals of 1980 (*Evita*), 1983 (*Cats*), 1988 (*The Phantom of the Opera*), and 1995 (*Sunset Boulevard*).

Men

"So, in Lady Chatterley's Lover we have a man, Sir Clifford, who is purely a personality, having lost entirely all connection with his fellow men and women, except those of usage. All warmth is gone entirely, the hearth is cold, the heart does not humanly exist. He is a pure product of our civilization, but he is the death of the great humanity of the world. He is kind by rule but he does not know what warm sympathy means. He is what he is. And he loses the woman of his choice." (Lawrence *circa* 1930).

D(avid). H(erbert Richards). Lawrence (1885–1930). English by birth, Lawrence spent many combined years in Italy and Southern France. His possibly best-known novels, *Sons and Lovers* (1913) and *Lady Chatterley's Lover* (1928), were widely reviled for their explicit language and portrayals of sexual relationships. However, Lawrence's insights into human sexuality—especially that of women—has been noted by men and women scholars alike.

Omens

"It's an ill-wind that brings nobody good." (Lawrence 1928).

Picking Leaders

"Its better to sail with a moody good captain than a laughing bad one." (Melville 1851).

Reading Fiction

"Fiction gives us an image of life—sometimes of a life we actually have and like to dwell on, but often and poignantly of one we have had and do not have now, or one we have never had and can never have." (Warren 1989).

Robert Penn Warren (1905–1989). One of the American South's great poets and novelists, Warren founded the *Southern Review* while a faculty member at Louisiana State University. Possibly best known for his Pulitzer prize-winning novel, *All the King's Men*, which is loosely based on the infamous life of Louisiana Governor Huey Long. *All the King's Men* was also the basis for the film of the same name that won an Academy Award for Best Picture of 1949.

Sea

Re Captain Nemo's monologue: "The sea is everything! . . . Its breathe is pure and wholesome. The sea is the immense desert where man is never alone, for he feels life pulsating all about him. The sea is nothing but the means which permits man to lead an almost supernatural existence; it is all movement and love." (Verne 1970).

Jules (Gabriel) Verne (1828–1905). Prolific French novelist best known for wonderfully engaging science fiction works such as *Voyage to the Center of the Earth* (1864), *Around the World in Eighty Days* (1873), and of course, *20,000 Leagues Under the Sea* (1870), all of which have been made into memorable films.

Twilight

"What a beautiful hour of the day is that of the twilight when things disappear and seem to melt into each other, and this great beautiful feeling of peace overshadows all." (Steichen 1991).

Edward Steichen (1879–1973). One of the twentieth century's great American artists, Steichen produced stunning photographs of the New York City environs. A significant number of his works portray city scenes in varying degrees of fog, haze, or icy mist. And, in many ways, these photographic works serve as metaphors for the ambiguity that is frequently experienced in life.

Water and the Sea

"Yes, as every one knows, meditation and water are wedded for ever." (Melville 1851).

Women and Women's Understanding

"I really like women better than men; they are braver, one can be more frank with them." (Lawrence 1928).

Youth

"Our first youth is of no value; for we are never conscious of it until after it is gone. But sometimes . . . there comes a sense of second youth gushing out of the heart's joy at being in love; or, possibly, it may come to crown some other grand festival in life, if any other such there be." (Hawthorne 1851).

Appendix Eight

Fair Use Provisions (Section 107) of the 1976 U.S. Copyright Act, As Amended—Relevant to Educational Use of Copyright Materials Considered for Use in Presentations

"§ 107. Limitations on exclusive rights: Fair use Notwithstanding the provisions of sections 106 and 106A [17 USC §§ 106, 106A] the fair use of a copyrighted work, including such use by reproduction in copies or phonorecords or by any other means specified by that section, for purposes such as criticism, comment, news reporting, teaching (including multiple copies for classroom use), scholarship, or research, is not an infringement of copyright. In determining whether the use made of a work in any particular case is a fair use the factors to be considered shall include:

(1) the purpose and character of the use, including whether such use is of a commercial nature or is for nonprofit educational purposes;
(2) the nature of the copyrighted work;
(3) the amount and substantiality of the portion used in relation to the copyrighted work as a whole; and
(4) the effect of the use upon the potential market for or value of the copyrighted work.

The fact that a work is unpublished shall not itself bar a finding of fair use if such finding is made upon consideration of all the above factors." http://www2.law.cornell.edu/cgi-bin/foliocgi.exe/copyrtact/query=*/doc/{@122}?

Appendix Nine

Sartorial Accessories and Related Allusions, References, or Themes Useful in Talks

Sartorial Accessories

Allusions, References, or Themes Useful in Talks

Academy Award Accessories

Lapel pins or neckties depicting Academy Award winners may be employed as "picking winners" accessories, which are useful for paying homage to the accomplishments of staff, students, faculty, or other professionals. My favorite accessories of this type are a necktie and lapel pin depicting Vivian Leigh and Clark Gable—stars of the 1939 David O. Selznick film, *Gone with the Wind*, which is based on Margaret Mitchell's best-selling novel of the same name. With these particular accessories, you can also point out the fact that *Gone with the Wind* was picked as the best picture of 1939 by the Academy of Motion Picture Arts and Sciences, in a year when the competition was extraordinary (the other 1939-entries included: *Dark Victory*, *Goodbye, Mr. Chips*, *Love Affair*, *Mr. Smith Goes to Washington*, *Ninotchka*, *Of Mice and Men*, *Stagecoach*, *The Wizard of Oz*, and *Wuthering Heights*). I also like to refer to Vivian Leigh's Oscar-winning performance in the Best Actress category along with Hattie McDaniel's Oscar for Best Supporting Actress, making her the first African-American woman to be accorded the honor. The lapel pin and necktie have also been used to segue into comments about *The Wizard of Oz* (see also, Leadership Accessories, below) because of this film's nomination in 1939.

Lapel pins and neckties embodying portraits or references to various Oscar winning actors, actresses, and films <http://www.oscars.org/> can be used in a parallel manner to the *Gone with the Wind* accessories. Pintreasures.com <http://www.pintreasures.com/> is a source of relevant lapel pins.

Awareness Ribbons and Facsimile Lapel Pins

Awareness ribbons and their lapel pin facsimiles can be worn and used to honor causes that may be embraced by audience members. The ribbons and their color connotations seem to multiply by the year, but following is a listing current during the first few years of the twenty-first century:

Black: Mourning
Black, Blue, Pink, and White: Childhood Mental Illness
Dark Blue: Child Abuse, Crime Victims' Rights, Education, Police
Light Blue: Pro-Choice
Blue, Red, and Yellow Jigsaw Puzzle Design: Autism
Blue and White Parallel Stripes: Israel
Gold: Childhood Cancer
Green: Environment, Organ Donor
Pink: Breast Cancer and Related Research
Rainbow: Diversity, Gay Pride, Multiculturalism
Red: Human Immunodeficiency Virus (HIV) and Acquired Immunodeficiency Syndrome (AIDS)
Red, White and Blue: U.S.A., 9-11
Violet: Abuse, Alzheimer's Disease, Anti-Violence, Domestic-Violence, Sarcoidosis
White: Child Abuse, Diabetes
White with Red Blotches: Chicken Pox
Yellow: Distant Loved One, Equality, Human Rights, Missing in Action (MIA), Prisoner of War (POW), Safe Return, Suicide Prevention

Awareness ribbons and facsimile lapel pins are available through the following Internet companies: Ribbons.Net <http://www.ribbons.net/index.html>, Pintreasures.com <http://www.pintreasures.com/>, and Sonoma Pins etc. <http://www.sonomapins.com/>.

Consilience Scarves and Ties

The Greek meander pattern (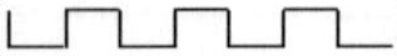), appears commonly on neckties and scarves, either as a main or auxiliary design. This pattern denotes the idea, "everlasting." It is also symbolic of Ariadne's threat, which allows reference to consilience (Wilson 1998) and the story of Theseus and the Minotaur as described in Chapter 5.

Escher Ties

The renowned Dutch artist, Maurits Cornelius Escher (more commonly referred to simply as M. C. Escher, [1898–1972]) created intricate works of art, several designs from which have been crafted into neckties. I particularly enjoy using the *Detail from Metamorphose II* (1939–40) tie, which contains imagery from a 7½ in. × 12 ft. 10 in. woodcut featuring a set of transitions from simple geometric to figurative to animal to architectural forms back to simple geometric forms. The portrayed literal and figurative metamorphoses are excellent metaphors for continuity in human intellectual development. An additional Escher tie, containing detail from *Another World II* (1947), embodies interwoven architectural elements and figurative representations of birds and horns. The architectural features provide metaphors for points about strength and renewal, while the bird and horn features symbolize harbingers or symbols of renewal. The artistic symbolism helps to make the point of the interconnectedness of study in the arts and sciences and integration of understanding that is sought through interdisciplinary study. A third Escher tie, *Fish and Insect* (1939), with creatures passing in opposite directions—a theme in many Escher works—provides an excellent symbol for the comings and goings of life. The figures in the tie—often seen differently—from near and far, offer symbolism for advice about looking at the "big picture" of life *versus* daily minutiae. Some of Escher's works, including *Metamorphose II* (in color) can be viewed at the Official M. C. Escher website, <http://www.mcescher.com/>.

Flag Accessories

Flag lapel pins and neckties can be used for various dramatic and intriguing allusions in talks. After September 11, 2001, U.S. patriotic lapel pins and neckties have become commonly available and useful in crafting comments. Flag lapel pins depicting all states in the U.S. and many foreign countries are available from Pintreasures.com <http://www.pintreasures.com/> and Sonoma Pins etc. <http://www.sonomapins.com/>. These companies are also good sources of friendship flag lapel pins, typically including flag representations of the U.S. and other nations or states.

Jerry Garcia Ties

Many people know that the deceased lead guitarist of the *Grateful Dead*, Jerry Garcia, was an accomplished musical artist. But, probably fewer people know that he was also an accomplished visual artist who worked in a variety of media including airbrush, digital, line drawings, ink, multi-media, and watercolors. Details from several of Garcia's works are now available in a Limited Edition Necktie Series. I have used his *Hummingbird* (an artistically and biologically stunning creature that serves as a metaphor for excellence in the arts and sciences) and *Paris in the Rain* (supporting references to France and French culture around the globe) ties for dramatic and intriguing allusions in talks. Another pattern, *Lady with Argyle Socks*—containing a modernistic version of Tartan art—can be used in allusions to Scottish history and related lore. Argyle—the Tartan specific for the Campbell Clan of a former western Scottish county known as Argyle or Argyll, typifies many Tartans with their interwoven checkered patterns. Audiences will be fascinated by the little known reason for Tartan kilts. Namely, empowering warriors with a facility to climb mountains and ford streams. This fact can be used for inspirational allusions. I also use the allusion of the bravery, wit, and heart of Scottish warriors (remember the movie, *Brave Heart*) as a model set of concepts for professional development.

One additional necktie, *Blue Mountain*, can be used in an appropriate setting to quote Alan Hovhaness (1911–2000), who once noted (relative to his Second Symphony—*Mysterious Mountain*), that "Mountains are natural meeting places for the mundane and spiritual worlds." For the more adventuresome and especially for colleagues who happen to be "deadheads," allusions can also be crafted among the Jerry Garcia tie imagery and song titles or lyrics made popular through the band's musical talents. Additional information about Jerry Garcia, his music and art can be found at the official *Grateful Dead* website, <http://www.dead.net/>.

Leadership Accessories

Ties can be purchased that contain triangular-shaped objects—sometimes associated with art deco designs. The triangular shapes can be used as symbols of the tripartite leadership model developed through references to the first OZ story and its three main characters, *viz*. the Scarecrow (intelligence), the Tin Woodman (love), and the Cowardly Lion (courage), as noted in Chapter 6. OZ lapel pins, including a depiction of the Scarecrow, Tin Woodman, and Cowardly Lion are available from Pintreasures.com <http://www.pintreasures.com/>.

Mackintosh Accessories

Charles Rennie Mackintosh (1868–1928), the great *fin d' siecle* Scottish architect and artist crafted beautiful designs that he incorporated into works of art, buildings, interior furnishings, and textiles (Swinglehurst 2001). Some of the designs also represented collaborations with his wife, Margaret Macdonald, her sister Francis, and their mutual friend, Herbert MacNair. There are three Mackintosh ties that I have found useful in presentations. The *Tulip and Lattice Design* and the *Chair, Rose and Washstand* ties contain typical Mackintosh art nouveau designs, but designs that seem very "modern" because of their timeless elements. When speaking before audiences familiar with architecture, linking the Mackintosh influence to the twentieth century designs of the great American architects, Frank Lloyd Wright and Faye Jones, provides a metaphor for the blending of the seasoned with the modern—whether they be designs, ideas, or values. The *Rose and Teardrop* necktie, incorporating a design used in art works both by Charles Rennie Mackintosh and Margaret Macdonald, represents the joys and pathos of life and the mixed feelings that inevitably permeate memorial events, as noted in Chapter 9. To view the art and other work of Charles Rennie Mackintosh, along with an array of accessories, try the Glasgow School of Art website, <http://www.gsa.ac.uk/mackintosh/>.

Map Ties

Neckties bearing maps are useful in talks of various types. The maps can be used to refer to a country or city that is relevant to a partnership that may be emerging between your firm, institution, or organization and that represented by members of an audience. A map tie containing depictions of your home town or city may also be useful in making points about childhood memories or memories you wish to have your audience consider regarding their early lives.

I have also used maps depicted in neckties as a metaphor for life's accomplishments. The intriguing notion is offered that one's life-map should take on the order and beauty we observe in maps of admired cities or other places. If the map also honors the origin of a person or persons noted in your remarks—then all the better. A case in point was a recent talk in which I used the story of Stephen Sondheim and his early tutoring by Oscar Hammerstein to illustrate the importance of teaching and mentoring in the lives of young scholars. The necktie map used in the talk was a facsimile of an 1852 map of New York City, chosen to honor Sondheim's birthplace.

William Morris Scarves and Ties

William Morris (1834–98) was a great English artist, author, craftsman, social critic and utopian dreamer, and key contributor to the Arts and Crafts Movement of the nineteenth century. Many of his original art works—frequently containing beautiful floral designs—are portrayed on neckties. The "Morris message" is one of multiple talents and a blending of the artistic and social—practical and aesthetic. These represent wonderful allusions for individuals and groups wishing to find new creative paths in their lives. The William Morris Society website (<http://www.morrissociety.org/>) has links to vendors of accessories incorporating William Morris designs. The Met Store at the Metropolitan Museum of Art in New York (<http://www.metmuseum.org/>) is also a source of William Morris design scarves.

Mosaic Scarves and Ties

The "power of mosaic"—as it may be referred to—is that of diversity and strength. Mosaic patterns can be found on neckties and if they represent classic works—all the better. The "mosaic message" is one of seeing patterns in different ways and through different perspectives. It is also the lesson of seeing differences "near and far" and appreciating the beauty of patterns from afar but understanding how important diverse elements are in lending beauty and strength. These allusions provide wonderful similes for comments about diversity in thought and among people in the workplace or other communities.

New Beginnings Ties

Many neckties can be found that incorporate egg-shaped objects. One of my "egg ties" is enhanced with the colors of spring and thus highlights the "new beginnings" allusion. There are many occasions when professionals are asked to speak about beginnings of causes, periods, or events. A "new beginnings" tie provides the reference for final comments based on the symbolism of the egg, and possible expressions of freshness, new hope, and renewed enthusiasm that may be hallmarks of a talk or activities among people within an firm, institution, or organization.

Ouroboros Scarves and Ties

In many cultures, the self-devouring serpent is used to symbolize creation, re-creation and the interrelatedness of all things—what we would call today, "consilience." In Egyptian and Greek lore, the term for this creature is "Ouroboros" and its use is probably most recognizable in the margin art of the Book of Kells—the *circa* ninth century illuminated manuscript of the Synoptic Gospels (Meehan 1995). This margin art is often found in neckties and scarves and the latter accessories are effectively used to emphasize points about the life-enriching value of scholarly and other creative pursuits.

Paisley Scarves and Ties

Paisley designs have roots in sixteenth century Central Asia, India, Persia, and most significantly, Kashmir. The paisley curvilinear teardrop design is inspired by plant forms especially those of the growing shoots of the date palm. Historians note that the date palm had economic importance (*e.g.*, food, fiber and shelter) to civilizations going back to the Babylonians who referred to the plant as the "Tree of Life" (Andrews 2003). In more modern times, paisley designs became popular motifs for shawls worn by women in European salons of the late eighteen through late nineteenth centuries. In the twentieth century, paisley designs became popularly incorporated into women's scarves and men's neckties. Paisley neck-ware, therefore, provides a rich source of historic, cultural, and metaphoric symbolism to craft a variety of allusions that enhance talks.

Tapestry Scarves and Ties

Tapestries are rich sources of symbols and meaning. Museum shops often offer for sale, neckties and scarves with depictions of tapestries—from either local or other collections. One on my favorite tapestry neckties contains detail of the Bayeux Tapestry, which is one of the greatest art works in Western Civilization. You may relish sharing a bit of the known history of this tapestry, particularly its unusual shape (231 feet long by 19½ in. wide), its depiction of life about the time of the Normal conquest of England (following the battle of Hastings in 1066 A.C.E.), and its likely creation by craftswomen. More importantly, the tie can be used to demonstrate an important aspect of leadership—especially for leaders who are newly joining firms, institutions, or organizations. For this allusion, one may go back to a bit of history and the fact that the Normans' impact on English culture was diminished because of the invaders' arrogance and tendency to insulate themselves from the English peasantry. You might also enjoy referring to a comment made by Alistair Cook some years ago when he stated that were it not for the arrogance of the Normans, Americans might now be speaking French! Herein lie important lessons for the novice in any firm, institution, or organization and sharing this story signals the significance a newcomer should place on recognizing the talents of his or her new colleagues.

A second tapestry tie I have used contains detail from a fourteenth century French tapestry, including lovely depictions of unicorns. With this imagery, one can make reference to the extensive use of unicorn symbolism in literature and heraldry from sources as diverse as British, Chinese, Greek, Hebrew, and Indian, the latter being a possible direct link *vis-à-vis* the Indian rhinoceros. This imagery and symbolism can be connected to present-day talks through literary associations of unicorns with power and protection from poison. Tapestry art also suggests allusions that can be made about attempts to modulate emphases on power and materialism through a love of aesthetics.

Tiffany Scarves and Ties

There are a variety of neck-ware produced that contain detail of the artwork—particularly stained glass work—of Louis Comfort Tiffany (1848–1933). Allusions to Tiffany and his work may include his being the son of Charles Louis Tiffany, the founder of Tiffany & Company in New York. More importantly, one can point to the myriad talents of Louis Comfort Tiffany, who not only worked in glass but also produced art works encompassing ceramic objects, jewelry, marble, paintings, and woodwork. Most notably, and here is where an interesting "hook" resides relative to talks on creativity and research, Tiffany's creations transcended the arts and sciences. Working with John La Farge, Tiffany developed "favrile" or uniquely colored and opalescent glasses and techniques (*e.g.*, the overlaying of glass pieces) for the crafting of unusually beautiful objects (*e.g.*, lamp shades, screens, windows, among others) (Frelinghuysen 1999). Thus, Tiffany was able to integrate understanding and skills across disciplinary barriers among the arts and sciences, well before interdisciplinary studies became common. The integration of talents and knowledge represent an important message that particularly blends well into talks embodying education or continuing education themes. The Met Store at the Metropolitan Museum of Art in New York <http://www.metmuseum.org/> is a source of Tiffany design scarves.

Appendix Ten

Example of Biographical Sketch for Use in Making Introductions

Bob Smith
Provost and Vice Chancellor for Academic Affairs
University of Arkansas, 422 Administration Building
Fayetteville, Ark. 72701 U.S.A.
tel.: 501-575-2151; fax: 501-575-7076
e-mail: bobsmith@comp.uark.edu
website: http://www.uark.edu/admin/vcacsey/

Bob Smith serves as Provost and Vice Chancellor for Academic Affairs at the University of Arkansas (U of A). Bob reports to the Chancellor and is the chief academic officer for the University. In this position, he has responsibility for academic affairs policy development and oversight of nine colleges and schools, along with several other academic units (e.g., Air Force and Army ROTC, the Teaching and Faculty Support Center, and the offices of institutional research and summer session).

Prior to joining the U of A, Bob served as Vice Provost for Research and Graduate Education and Dean of the Graduate School at the University of Connecticut (UConn). In this position, Bob had responsibility for research oversight at Storrs and the regional campuses and graduate education across the UConn system, including biomedical graduate programs at the Health Center in Farmington.

Before assuming the post at UConn, Bob served for ten years as Vice Provost for Research and Dean of the Graduate School at Washington State University (WSU). Also at WSU, Bob served as Dean of the College of Pharmacy during 1985–86. Bob's earlier academic and administrative appointments included serving as James E. Bauerle Professor (1983–85) and Director of the Drug

Dynamics Institute (1978–85) at the University of Texas at Austin (UT Austin). He also served in Professor (1977–83) and Associate Professor (1974–77) positions at UT Austin. He began his academic career at the University of Iowa where he was Associate and Assistant Professor of Medicinal Chemistry (1968–74). Bob's Ph.D. (1968) and master's (1964) degrees (Pharmaceutical Chemistry) were earned at the University of Michigan; his B.S. degree (Pharmaceutical Sciences) was awarded by St. John's University in New York (1963). Bob is a native of New York. His research and scholarly interests have been in the pharmaceutical sciences, communication, professional development, and university administration. He is the author or co-author of over 240 published articles and five books, including *The Elements of Great Speechmaking: Adding Drama & Intrigue*, which was published by University Press of America in 2004.

Bob Smith was profiled in the February 4, 2001 edition of the *Arkansas Democrat Gazette*, pp. D-1 and D-4.

Bibliography

Allen, Woody. *Annie Hall*. Los Angeles: MGM/UA Studios, 1977.

Andrews, Meg. *Victoriana.com Study Center*. 2003. <http://www.victoriana.com/library/paisley/shawl.html>.(15 Jul. 2003)

Andrews, Robert, Mary Biggs, and Michael Seidel, ed. *The Columbia World of Quotations*. CD-ROM. New York: Columbia University Press, *circa* 1996.

Armstrong, Eddie, Personal Communication, 2000.

Artchive. Roy Lichtenstein. 2003. <http://www.artchive.com/artchive/L/lichtenstein.html> (10 Jul. 2003)

Art Institute of Chicago, Chicago, Ill. Grant Wood. *American Gothic*. 2003. <http://www.artic.edu/aic/collections/modern/73mac_wood.html> (10 Jul. 2003)

Austen, Jane. *Pride and Prejudice*. Afterword by Joann Morse. New York: Penguin, 1980; first published in 1813.

Bartlett, John and Justin Kaplan, ed. *Bartlett's Familiar Quotations: A Collection of Passages, Phrases, and Proverbs Traced to Their Sources in Ancient and Modern Literature*. 17th ed. New York: Little, Brown & Co., 2002.

Baum, L. Frank. *The Wizard of OZ*. New York: Puffin Books, 1982; first published in 1900.

Baum, L. Frank. *The Annotated Wizard of OZ—The Wonderful Wizard of OZ*. Pictures by W. W. Denslow. Introduction, notes, and bibliography by Michael Patrick Hearn. New York: Crown, 1973.

Beckett, Sister Wendy. *Sister Wendy's American Collection*. Toby Eady Associates, ed. New York: HarperCollins, 2000.

Berg, A. Scott. *Lindbergh*. New York: G. P. Putnam's Sons, 1998.

Beveridge, W. I. B. *The Art of Scientific Investigation*. 3d ed. New York: Vintage, 1957.

Boller, Paul F. and John George. *They Never Said It—A Book of Fake Quotes, Misquotes, and Misleading Attributions*. New York: Oxford University Press, 1989.

Brantley, Ben, ed. *The New York Times Book of Broadway*. New York: New York Times, 2001.

Brodie, Fawn. *Thomas Jefferson—An Intimate History*. New York: Norton, 1974.

Brokaw, Tom. *The Greatest Generation*. New York: Random House, 1998.

Buscaglia, Leo. *Living, Loving & Learning*. New York: Fawcett Columbine, 1982.

Campbell, Joseph. *The Hero with a Thousand Faces*. 2d ed. Princeton, N.J.: Princeton University Press, 1968.

Carre, John le. *Tinker, Tailor, Soldier, Spy*. New York: Knopf, 1974.

Carroll, Lewis. *Alice's Adventures in Wonderland*. New York: Penguin, 1960; first published in 1865.

Carroll, Lewis. *Through the Looking Glass and What Alice Found There*. New York: Penguin, 1960; first published in 1872.

Carroll, Lewis. *Alice's Adventures Under Ground*. Forward by Mary Jean St Clair (Alice Liddell's granddaughter). London: Pavilion, 1985.

Cartledge, Paul, ed. *The Cambridge Illustrated History of Ancient Greece*. New York: Cambridge University Press, 1998.

Ceram, C. W. *Gods, Graves, and Scholars*. 2d ed. New York: Knopf, 1982.

Church, F. Forrester. "The eclectic Forrester Church." *The World* 2, no. 3 (May/June 1988): 21–23.

Clark, Anne. *Lewis Carroll—A Biography*. New York: Schocken Books, 1979.

Clooney, Nick. *The Movies That Changed Us*. New York: Atria Books, 2002.

Coles, Robert. *The Call of Stories—Teaching and the Moral Imagination*. Boston: Houghton Mifflin, 1989.

Commencement Booklet. Storrs, Conn.: University of Connecticut, 1999.

Cook, Alistair. *Six Men*. New York: Berkley, 1977.

Cook, Jeff Scott. *The Elements of Speechwriting and Public Speaking*. New York: Macmillan, 1989.

Davis, Allen F. *American Heroine—The Life and Legend of Jane Addams*. Chicago: Ivan R. Dee, 2000.

Dean, Fletcher. "Tips of the Trade—Writing Great Titles." *OnSpeechwriting* 3, no. 4/5 (May 2003). <fletcher@thespeechwriter.com> (6 May 2003).

Detz, Joan. *How to Write and Give a Speech*. New York: St. Martin's Griffin, 1992.

Detz, Joan. *It's Not What You Say, It's How You Say It*. New York: St. Martin's Griffin, 2000.

Diamond, Jared. *Guns, Germs, and Steel—The Fates of Human Societies*. New York: Norton, 1997.

Dickinson, Emily. *The Selected Poems of Emily Dickinson*. New York: The Modern Library, 1996.

Dostoyevsky, Fyodor. *The Idiot*. Constance Garnett, trans. New York: Dell, 1959; first published in 1869.

Duncan, Dayton and Ken Burns. *Lewis & Clark—The Journey of the Corps of Discovery*. New York: Knopf, 1997.

Eiseley, Loren. *The Immense Journey*. New York: Vintage, 1957.

Flexner, Eleanor and Ellen Fitzpatrick. *A Century of Progress—The Woman's Rights Movement in the United States*. Cambridge: Harvard University Press, 1996.

Fontana, David. *The Secret Language of Symbols—A Visual Key to Symbols and Their*

Meanings. San Francisco: Chronicle Books, 1993.

Foote, Shelby. *The Civil War: A Narrative: Fort Sumter to Perryville, Fredericksburg to Meridian, Red River to Appomattox*. Vols. 1–3. New York: Vintage Books, 1986.

Franklin, Benjamin. *Poor Richard of his almanacs* (written under the pseudonym of Richard Saunders); first published *circa* 1757.

Frelinghuysen, Alice Cooney. *Louis Comfort Tiffany at the Metropolitan Museum of Art*. New Haven, Conn.: Yale University Press, 1999.

Gibson, Chere Campbell. "Distance Education—Challenges/Opportunities." Paper presented at the Arkansas Distance Education Conference, Fayetteville, Ark., Jan. 2002.

Gilchrist, Ellen. *The Cabal and Other Stories*. New York: Little, Brown & Co., 2000.

Gray, Donald J. *Alice in Wonderland—Authoritative Texts of Alice's Adventures in Wonderland, Through the Looking Glass, The Hunting of the Snark, Backgrounds, and Essays in Criticism*. 2d ed. New York: Norton, 1992.

Grunwald, Henry. "Home is Where You Are Happy." *Time* 126, no. 1 (8 Jul. 1985): 100–101.

Hale, Harrison. *University of Arkansas 1871–1948*. Fayetteville, Ark.: University of Arkansas Alumni Association, 1948.

Hawking, Stephen. *A Brief History of Time*. New York: Bantam Books, 1988.

Hawking, Stephen. *The Universe in a Nutshell*. New York: Bantam Books, 2001.

Hawthorne, Nathaniel. *The House of the Seven Gables*. New York: Bantam Books, 1981; first published in 1851.

Heyerdahl, Thor. *Early Man and the Ocean: A Search for the Beginnings of Navigation and Seaborne Civilizations*. New York: Doubleday, 1979.

Heyerdahl, Thor and F. H. Lyon. *Kon-Tiki: Across the Pacific by Raft*. New York: Washington Square Press, 1995; first published in 1950.

Heyerdahl, Thor. *In the Footsteps of Adam: A Memoir*. Toronto: Warwick Publishers, 2002.

Homer. *The Iliad*. Stanley Lombardo, trans. Indianapolis, Ind.: Hackett, 1997; first published *circa* 900–800 B.C.E.

Homer. *The Odyssey*. Stanley Lombardo, trans. Indianapolis, Ind.: Hackett, 2000; first published *circa* 900–800 B.C.E.

Hornung, Erik and Betsy M. Bryan, ed. *The Quest for Immortality—Treasures of Ancient Egypt*. Wash. D.C. and Copenhagen: National Gallery of Art and United Exhibits Group, 2002.

Hoving, Thomas and Andrew Wyeth. *Art for Dummies*. New York: For Dummies, 1999.

IdeaBank®, database of quotations, anecdotes, book and speech excerpts, proverbs, humor, and other material. <http://www.idea-bank.com/ib/html/index.html> (8 Jul. 2003).

Jaffe, Irma B. *Joseph Stella*. New York: Fordham University Press, 1988.

James, Henry. *The Bostonians*. New York: Penguin, 1986; first published in 1886.

Jaynes, Julian. *The Origin of Consciousness in the Breakdown of the Bicameral Mind*. Boston: Houghton Mifflin, 1976.

Jeary, Tony. *Inspire Any Audience—Proven Secrets of the Pros for Powerful Presen-*

tations. Tulsa, Okla.: Trade Life, 1997.

Jung, C. G. *Memories, Dreams, Reflections*. Aniela Jaffé, ed. Richard and Clara Winston, trans. New York: Vintage Books, 1965.

Kennedy, Paul M. *The Rise and Fall of the Great Powers: Economic Change and Military Conflict from 1500 to 2000*. New York: Random House, 1987.

Kimbell Art Museum, Fort Worth, Tex. Louis-Léopold Boilly. *The Geography Lesson*. 2003. http://www.kimbellart.org/database/index.cfm?detail=yes&ID=AP%201990.01 (10 Jul. 2003)

Kurian, George, ed. *A Historical Guide to the U.S. Government*. New York: Oxford University Press, 1998.

Koshland, Jr., Daniel. "Retire or Not to Retire, That is the Question." *Science* 239, no. 4842 (19 Feb. 1988): 845.

Lawrence, D. H. *Lady Chatterley's Lover*. The Unexpurgated 1928 Orioli Edition. New York: Bantam, 1968; including *A Propos of Lady Chatterley's Lover*, *circa* 1930.

Levinson, Jay A., ed. *Circa 1492—Art in the Age of Exploration*. Washington, D.C.: National Gallery of Art and New Haven, Conn.: Yale University Press, 1991.

Making the Case—The Impact of The University of Arkansas on the Future of the State of Arkansas. First report of the 2010 Commission. Fayetteville, Ark.: University of Arkansas, 2001.

Mandela, Nelson. *Long Walk to Freedom—The Autobiography of Nelson Mandela*. New York: Little, Brown & Co., 1994.

Maugham, W. Somerset. *The Razor's Edge*. Introduction by Anthony Curtis. New York: Penguin, 1992; first published in 1944.

McCabe, Terry. "Stephen Sondheim: Exploring Our Myths." *Chronicle of Higher Education* 48, no. 35 (10 May 2002): B18.

McCollough, David. *John Adams*. New York: Simon & Schuster, 2001.

McCourt, Frank. *Angela's Ashes—A Memoir*. New York: Scribner, 1996.

McCourt, Frank. *'Tis—A Memoir*. New York: Scribner, 1999.

McMullen, Roy Donald. "Wassily Kandinsky." *Encyclopædia Britannica Online*. 2001. <http://search.eb.com/eb/article?eu=45572> (2 July 2001).

McGuire, Jack. *The Power of Personal Storytelling*. New York: Jeremy P. Tarcher/Putnam, 1998.

McPherson, James M. *Battle Cry of Freedom—The Civil War Era*. New York: Oxford University Press, 1988.

Meehan, Bernard. *The Book of Kells: An Illustrated Introduction to the Manuscript in Trinity College Dublin*. 2d ed. New York: Thames & Hudson, 1995.

Melville, Herman. *Moby Dick*. New York: Bantam Books, 1981; first published in 1851.

Morris, William. *News from Nowhere; or, An Epoch of Rest*. New York: Monthly Review Press, 1966; first published in 1890.

Müller, F. Max, trans. *The Upanishads*. Oxford: Clarendon Press, 1879–84; first published *circa* 700–500 B.C.E.

Nanda, Bal Ram. *Mahatma Gandhi: A Biography*. New York: Oxford University Press, 1992.

Nasar, Sylvia. *A Beautiful Mind*. New York: Simon & Shuster, 1994.

National Gallery. Washington, D. C. Thomas Cole. *The Voyage of Life*. 2003. <http://www.nga.gov/cgi-bin/pinfo?Object=52167+0+none> (10 Jul. 2003)

Nelson-Atkins Museum of Art, Kansas City, Mo. Alberto Giacometti. *The Chariot*. 2003. <http://www.nelson-atkins.org/collections/20thcent/detail/chariot.htm> (10 Jul. 2003)

Nevis, Allan and Henry Graff. "George Washington." *Encyclopædia Britannica Online*. 2002. <http://search.eb.com/eb/article?eu=115703> (15 Nov. 2002)

The Oxford Dictionary of Quotations. 5th ed. Los Angeles: Getty Center for Education in the Arts, 1999.

Peck, M. Scott. *The Road Less Traveled*. New York: Simon & Schuster, 1978.

Perlman, Alan M. *Writing Great Speeches—Professional Techniques You Can Use*. Boston: Allyn and Bacon, 1998.

Questia. An online library containing more than 400,000 books, journals, and articles (in 2003). <http://www.questia.com/Index.jsp> (1 Jul. 2003).

Ratcliff, Susan, ed. *People on People—The Oxford Dictionary of Quotations*, New York: Oxford University Press, 2001. (and many permutations thereof; see *Books in Print*)

Robinson, Grady Jim. *"Did I Ever Tell You the One About the Time . . . "*. New York: McGraw-Hill, 2000.

Robinson, Grady Jim. *"Find the Victory"*. Audiotapes. Fayetteville, Ark.: Grady Jim Robinson, 2001.

Rostow, W. W. *The Barbaric Counterrevolution: Cause and Cure*. Austin: University of Texas Press, 1983.

Rothko, Mark. Commentary from the Art Institute of Chicago found at the National Gallery of Art, Wash. DC website. 2003. <http://www.nga.gov/feature/rothko/classic5.html> (15 Jun. 2001).

Sagan, Carl. *Broca's Brain*. New York: Ballantine, 1974.

Sagan, Carl. *The Dragons of Eden—Speculations on the Evolution of Human Intelligence*, New York: Ballantine, 1977; reissued in 1989.

Sagan, Carl. *Contact*. New York: Pocket Books, 1985.

Saint Exupéry, Antoine de. *The Little Prince*. New York: Harcourt, Brace & World, 1943.

Scarry, Richard. *Cars and Trucks and Things That Go*. New York: Golden Press, 1974. (and many other titles)

Seldes, George, ed. *The Great Quotations*. Secaucus, N.J.: The Citadel Press, 1983.

Seldes, George, ed. *The Great Thoughts*, New York: Crown, 1994.

Sheehan, J. C. *The Enchanted Ring. The Untold Story of Penicillin*. Cambridge: MIT Press, 1982.

Shelley, Mary Wollstonecroft. *Frankenstein*. Introduction by Robert E. Dowse and D. J. Palmer. New York: Dutto, 1963; first published in 1818.

Smith, Robert V. *Development and Management of Research Groups—A Guide for University Researchers*. Austin: University of Texas Press, 1980; 2d ed. published as *Development and Management of University Research Groups*. Austin: University of Texas Press, 1986.

Smith, Robert V. and Thomas F. George. "Winds of Change are Buffeting Higher Education's Tower of Research." *Universe* (Research Magazine of Washington State University), 7 no. 1 (Spring 1994): 22–26; see also, Robert V. Smith. "American Universities Need to Lead Way into the Future." *Oregonian 142*, no. 47,504 (10 Feb. 1993): C-7.

Smith, Robert V. *Graduate Research—A Guide for Students in the Sciences*. 3d ed. Seattle: University of Washington Press, 1998.

Smith, Robert V. "There Will Never be Another You: Personal Recollections of Bob Gray—Connecticut's Lost Treasure." *Papers from the Memorial Celebration for Robert V. Gray*. Storrs, Conn.: University of Connecticut School of Fine Arts, 1999.

Smith, Bob. "The Power of Heliotrope." *Arkansas* (Magazine of the Arkansas Alumni Association) 51, no. 2 (Winter 2001): 24–25.

Spitz, Ellen Handler. "The Magical Neighborhood of Mr. Rogers." *Chronicle of Higher Education* 49, no. 29 (28 Mar. 2003): B-16.

Steichen, Edward. From the exhibit, "Night Life." San Diego, Calif.: Museum of Photographic Art, 1991.

Swainson, Bill. *Encarta® Book of Quotations*. New York: St. Martin's Press, 2000.

Swinglehurst, Edmund. *Charles Rennie Mackintosh*. San Diego, Calif.: Thunder Bay Press, 2001.

Thoreau, Henry David. *Walden*. Introduction and editing by Joseph Wood Krutch. New York: Bantam Books, 1962; first published in 1854.

Tocqueville, Alexis De. *Democracy in America*. Vols. I and II. Charlottesville: University of Virginia. 2002; first published in 1835. <http://xroads.virginia.edu/~HYPER/DETOC/home.html> (1 Sept. 2002).

Tuchman, Barbara. *The Guns of August*. New York: Ballantine, 1994.

Udall, Morris K. *Too Funny to be President*. New York: Holt, 1988.

Verne, Jules. *20,000 Leagues Under the Sea*. Mendor T. Brunetti, trans. New York: Penguin, 1969; first published in 1870.

Ward, Geoffrey C., Ric Burns, and Ken Burns. *The Civil War: An Illustrated History*, New York: Knopf, 1990.

Warren, Robert Penn. "On Reading Fiction." *Chronicle of Higher Education* 36, no. 5 (4 Oct. 1989): B64.

Webber, Andrew Lloyd. *Aspects of Love*. Musical. 1990.

Whelan, Bilkis. *Vastu in 10 Simple Lessons*. New York: Watson-Guptill, 2002.

White, T. H. *The Once and Future King (containing The Sword in the Stone, The Queen of Air and Darkness, The Ill-Made Knight, and The Candle in the Wind)*. New York: Putnam, 1958.

White, Virginia P. *Grants—How to Find Out About Them and What to do Next*. New York: Plenum Press, 1975.

Williams, Roger L. *The Origins of Federal Support for Higher Education*. University Park: The Pennsylvania State University Press, 1991.

Wilson, E. O. *Consilience—The Unity of Knowledge*. New York: Knopf, 1998.

Woods, Randall Bennett. *Fulbright—A Biography*. New York: Cambridge University

Press, 1995.

The World Factbook 2002. Washington, D.C.: U. S. Central Intelligence Agency, Office of Public Affairs. 2002. <http://www.odci.gov/cia/publications/factbook/index.html> (15 Aug. 2002).

Yagoda, Ben. "Quote, Unquote." *Chronicle of Higher Education* 48, no. 19 (18 Jan. 2002): B18.

Zachary, G. Pascal. *Endless Frontier: Vannevar Bush, Engineer of the American Century*. New York: Free Press, 1997.

Index

About the Author

Bob Smith has crafted a career serving U.S. higher education—as a faculty member and administrator—at the Universities of Arkansas, Iowa, Texas at Austin and Connecticut (UConn), along with Washington State University (WSU). Currently, he is serving as Provost and Vice Chancellor for Academic Affairs (second in command) at the University of Arkansas (U of A) in Fayetteville. Bob began his career in pharmaceutical education but during the past 15 years has held posts as chief research officer and graduate dean (WSU and UConn) and chief academic officer (U of A). He holds M.S. and Ph.D. degrees from the University of Michigan where he has since been recognized as one of 50 Distinguished Doctoral Graduates of the Horace H. Rackham School of Graduate Studies (1987) and Distinguished Alumnus of the College of Pharmacy (1990).

Bob is the author or co-author of over 240 publications and five books, including *Graduate Research—A Guide for Students in the Sciences*, which was published in a 3rd edition in 1998. During his career, Bob has served on many boards (e.g., Council of Graduate Schools Board of Directors, Graduate Record Exam Board, Washington Research Foundation Board of Directors) and executive committees (e.g., Executive Committee of Graduate Deans of The Africa-America Institute). He has also served as a consultant to universities and private industry, including Rutgers University, the University of Utah, and Wayne State University, Hoechst-Roussel Pharmaceuticals Inc., Hoffmann-LaRoche Inc., E. R. Squibb and Sons, and the Upjohn Co. All of his professional affiliations have resulted in hundreds of speaking engagements throughout the United States and in more than 22 other countries on every continent in the world, save Australia and Antarctica.

Bob has made presentations before professional and service organizations, legislative committees, university and foundation governance and advisory boards, faculty and higher educational administrative officials, college-age student and parent groups, primary and secondary students and teachers, and business and economic development groups. These hundreds of speaking engagements in a variety of venues have been testing grounds for the successful public speaking approaches and methods described in *EGS*.

Bob lives on the Ozark Plateau in Fayetteville with his artist wife Marsha June and their French bulldog Monsieur Hercule Poirot.